The Pura Belpré Award

1996–2016

20 Years of Outstanding Latino Children's Literature

"Through the power of a story and the beauty of language, the child escapes to a world of his own. He leaves the room richer than when he entered."

—Pura Belpré, *The Stories I Read to the Children*

ROSEN PUBLISHING

ACKNOWLEDGMENTS

This book has been made possible thanks to many people, but especially thanks to all our contributors, who so generously shared their personal journeys and experiences as writers, illustrators, and winners of the Pura Belpré Award for the past twenty years. Special thanks to the publishing committee, for this project: Oralia Garza de Cortés, Rita Auerbach, Ruth Tobar, Lucía González, Katie Scherrer, and Christine Dengel. Thanks to the editorial and design staff at Rosen, and to my collaborator and coeditor, Nathalie Beullens-Maoui, for helping with the project in so many different ways. To the publishers and literary agents for their continuous support and for their assistance in helping us connect with all the contributors. And finally, to Roger Rosen, president and CEO of Rosen Publishing, for his insight and for embracing this project, which will make it possible for millions of Latino children in the United States to feel proud of their heritage.

—Teresa Mlawer

Published in 2016 by The Rosen Publishing Group, Inc.
29 East 21st Street, New York, NY 10010

Compilation © 2016 The Rosen Publishing Group, Inc.

Book Cover and Photo Credits: Pages 110–112
Editorial Directors: Teresa Mlawer, Nathalie Beullens-Maoui.
Editors: Meredith Day, Jacob Steinberg
Book Design: Brian Garvey
ISBN: 9781499464344

Library of Congress Catalog-in Publication Data

Names: Beullens-Maoui, Nathalie.
Title: The Pura Belpré Award, 1996–2016: 20 Years of Outstanding Latino Children's Literature. / edited by Nathalie Beullens-Maoui and Teresa Mlawer.
Description: New York : Rosen Publishing, 2016. | Includes index.
Identifiers: ISBN 9781499464344 (library bound)
Subjects: LCSH: Belpré Medal--Bio-bibliography. | American literature-- Hispanic American authors --Awards. | Children's literature, American--Awards. | Hispanic Americans in literature--Bibliography. | Hispanic American authors--Biography.
Classification: LCC Z1037.A2 P87 2016 | DDC 810.99282079--dc23

Printed in the United States of America

CONTENTS

INTRODUCTION

Twenty years ago, we came together to carve out an inclusive vision for a literary America that included Latino children's authors and illustrators whose very heritage, and cultural experiences would serve to enrich a multicultural, multilingual society.

Our vision was a bold yet long overdue idea, born from a sense of injustice of the countless stories left unpaged. We were encountering teachers, writers, and artists who lamented their inability to get relevant stories into their students' hands and get their own stories published, and countless histories and childhood experiences were not reflected in those windows they opened when they found a book. Our dogged persistence and determination drove us to right a wrong, to insist that this long overdue literature be published, produced, honored and recognized, and hold its rightful place in the annals of literary children's history. We were joined by Linda Perkins, former president of ALSC, the Association of Library Services to Children, and Toni Bissessar, former president of REFORMA, the National Association to Promote Library and Information Services to Latinos and the Spanish Speaking, who suggested the award be named after Pura Belpré. Belpré was the first Latina librarian from the New York Public Library, a powerful legend and symbol of the importance of storytellers to tell one's own stories. Together, these library leaders embraced the vision and worked in unison to create a permanent space within the American Library Association (ALA), thus insuring the Belpré Award into perpetuity.

The collective passion and the groundswell of support that grew within the profession and with each passing year contributed to the transformation of children's literature as we know it now.

Latino and Latina illustrators and authors are now named at the ALA Youth Media Awards press conference. The dais at the ALA Annual Conference's Pura Belpré award ceremony—La Celebración—now reflects the diversity of Latino and Latina heritage as part of our literary America. Twenty years of the Pura Belpré Award has resulted in a more equitable, more fair, more just, more complete literature for all children, all families, all students, and all communities.

With this book, dear reader, you will enter the world of the very best of Latino children's literature. Be dazzled by the gift of story and art that graces the pages of these incredible works of art. Celebrate these works! Share these books, buy these books, and promote these books.

Happy 20th Birthday Pura Belpré Award!

—Oralia Garza de Cortés and Sandra Ríos Balderrama
Cofounders, the Pura Belpré Award

2016 Narrative Medal Winner

Margarita Engle

Enchanted Air

I was astonished and thrilled to learn that *Enchanted Air* will receive the 2016 Pura Belpré Medal at the 20th Anniversary Celebración! This book is a memoir so personal that writing it was both painful and medicinal. I can't change history, but the Pura Belpré Award can change the way my life story is perceived. It can also dramatically increase the number of young readers who will find *Enchanted Air* in their libraries and schools. All I did is share memories and emotions, but the award is confirmation that memories and emotions matter.

All our life stories are important. Only by learning about each other can we develop empathy, which is the first step toward peace. Imagine how wonderful it will be if teachers see the Pura Belpré Award seal on a memoir and decide to use it to help students write about their own lives! Imagine how wonderful it will be if some of those students go on to become writers, educators, and librarians, carrying the message that life stories matter far into the future.

More than any of my other books, *Enchanted Air* speaks directly about the immigration experience, which has so many universal aspects, even in the second generation. Of course, Latino authors don't just write for Latino readers. We write for all young people. I hope my true tale of a family limited by history will speak to anyone who has ever felt like an outsider for any reason.

I hope *Enchanted Air* will show how desperately we need mutual understanding and peace, in this new era when—just as during the Cold War—certain groups are singled out by politicians and the media for hatred, fear, and distrust. I feel certain that this profoundly significant recognition by the Pura Belpré committee will help my book reach young readers who are the only possible peacemakers of the future.

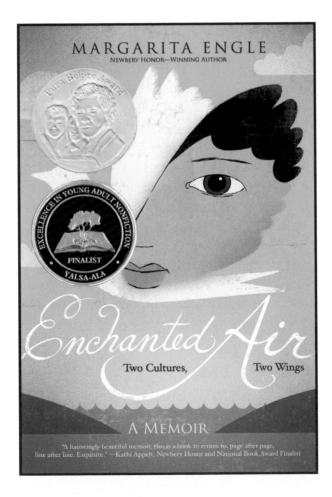

2016 Illustration Medal Winner

Rafael López

Drum Dream Girl

For twenty years, a medal that bears her name has given voice to Latino artists and writers by honoring the aspirations of children to see themselves in the pages of books. Words and pictures are not enough to express what it means to me to win the Pura Belpré Illustration Award on this anniversary year. It's gratitude that lifts me up, encourages me to keep taking chances, and affirms my desire to make a difference with my work.

I'm convinced that if Pura met Millo Castro Zaldarriaga, the heroine of *Drum Dream Girl*, they would have been good friends. These two determined women shared courage and imagination, daring to change hearts and minds. Millo's passion and perseverance broke Cuba's traditional taboo against female drummers, helping the next generation impact the future. Pura's originality and advocacy for the Spanish-speaking community through bilingual story hours and inventive programming transformed the 115th Street Branch Library into a New York center of culture. Agents of change, they broke barriers and challenged the status quo.

Surely planets aligned when I was given the chance to work with Margarita Engle, who crafts magnetic stories about independent thinkers. Her rhythmic, poetic style gave me the freedom to invent, evoking surrealistic ideas to channel the spirit of the *Drum Dream Girl* text.

I consider myself the lucky son of a dreamer. Despite resistance and challenge, my mother worked several jobs in order to secretly attend university and pursue her passion. She was in the first generation of female architects in Mexico City, entering a male-dominated profession in a traditional culture. Energized by her, I grew up making music, reading books about distant locations, drawing, and dreaming.

I'm deeply grateful to REFORMA. Thank you, Pura, for magnifying our diverse voices and daring us to dream.

2016 Honor Books for Narrative

Mango, Abuela, and Me
Meg Medina

Years ago, when my grandmother arrived from Cuba, she came with little more than the clothes on her back and a head full of stories. One of my favorites was about a parrot she had left behind, a colorful *loro* that could say "*buenos días*" to all the neighbors. I bought Abuela what I thought was a replacement at Woolworth's one day, but that little green bird never did say a word to us. Still, I never forgot meeting Abuela for the first time or the jaunty parrot that lived in her memory.

Mango, Abuela, and Me is about how we learn to become a family—even when we have to work at finding the universal language of love.

The Smoking Mirror
David Bowles

My children and I have read many fantasy series together: Narnia, Harry Potter, Percy Jackson, etc. But as a Latino father of Latino children, I yearned to open the pages of a YA novel and find Latino teens facing off against Mesoamerican deities and *cucuys* while dealing with issues plaguing our communities. One day it hit me—I wanted to be the one to write it. *The Smoking Mirror* emerged from that realization. I was giddy and grateful when it was selected as a Belpré Honor Book. The validation that comes from this unexpected recognition is truly momentous and humbling.

2016 Honor Books for Illustration

Funny Bones
Duncan Tonatiuh

El Día de Muertos, or the Day of the Dead, is a very special holiday in which people remember their loved ones who have passed away. Rather than being a sad and somber affair, the occasion is festive and colorful. Guadalupe Posada's *calaveras*, or skeleton drawings, have become synonymous with el Día de Muertos. His calaveras capture perfectly the sentiment of the festivity. I'm very happy that the Belpré committee honored *Funny Bones*. It will encourage young readers to learn about Don Lupe Posada—a wonderful yet largely unknown artist—and the Day of the Dead, a life-affirming holiday.

Mango, Abuela, and Me
Angela Dominguez

When I received my second Pura Belpré Illustration Honor for *Mango, Abuela, and Me*, I had to pinch myself. I couldn't believe it had happened again! To be recognized as an illustrator by my own community out of all the amazing books is incredible and astonishing. I have to thank Meg Medina. This honor couldn't possibly have happened without her beautiful words. They were so heartfelt and honest. They inspired me as I worked on the book from the sketches to the final artwork. I'm so pleased that the entire book resonates with people. I am truly grateful for the honor. Gracias!

My Tata's Remedies/Los remedios de mi tata
Antonio Castro

When Cinco Puntos offered me the chance to illustrate *My Tata's Remedies*, I was excited because my own grandmother used traditional medicine. If my legs ached, Abuela would wrap them with herbs soaked in rubbing alcohol. Tata's story also made me remember my grandparents' home, which was marked by warm hospitality. I reflected on those things as I was illustrating, trying with each image to show the love and generosity that is such a part of our Mexican culture. It was a rich pleasure to illustrate this book. Imagine my delight to be doubly rewarded with the Pura Belpré Award!

2015 Narrative Medal Winner

Marjorie Agosín

I Lived on Butterfly Hill

I was born in Bethesda, Maryland, in the middle of the summer. When I was an infant my family moved to Chile. My mother always told me I was really born in the winter because I belonged much more to the South of the world than to the North. I also belong to the country that nurtured me to become a poet: Chile, that long and narrow stretch of land almost at the end of the world. And to the port city of Valparaíso that gave my family refuge as they were escaping the Nazis. My novel *I Lived on Butterfly Hill* takes place in this luminous port city. I wanted my readers to love its whimsical ways the way I did as a young child.

The years went by, and eventually we returned to the U.S. We moved to Athens, Georgia, when I was fourteen years old. The North has now become my home and the place where I write about Chile, the place where I grew up. I live in the North but I also live in the South, and somehow I am grateful for both worlds. This is what I try to evoke in my writings.

Celeste Marconi, the protagonist of *I Lived on Butterfly Hill*, shows us that one can belong to all one loves. The spirit of my first young adult novel guided me to show my readers that in times of great adversity we find the resilience to continue pursuing our dreams and encounter possibilities that these new circumstances bring us.

I wanted to inspire Latino children to embrace the richness of their experiences, to be proud of their heritage, never to forget their past. Often our Latino community suffers from invisibility and neglect. Unfortunately, we do not have too many young characters to show us the way. Celeste Marconi is such a character. It is my hope that Latino children would be inspired by this young girl, by her fierce determination and by the belief that under adversity one can grow and change the world.

At the end of *I Lived on Butterfly Hill*, Celeste imagines that she can reunite her missing parents who were among Chile's disappeared and also reunite her country. I believe that we, as a Latino community, can also reunite our past and our present and realize our future. We are all a luminous patchwork of multiple identities. I hope the wisdom and the strength that Celeste carries with her will inspire us not to fear our own truth and to became doers and dreamers.

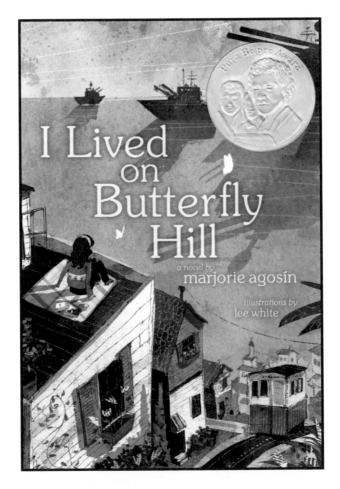

Yuyi Morales

Viva Frida

One day, when I was a kid, I sat next to my father, who was watching the movie *Frida, Naturaleza Viva*. The movie was dark and strange. I knew a little bit about Frida Kahlo because, like her, I did a lot of practicing my drawing by going inside my room and looking in the mirror. But learning how to draw the lines and shapes of my own face also made me feel self-conscious, for it seemed an act of narcissism that I was seldom brave enough to admit. Yet, I remember a tingling of validation when I learned about all those self-portraits that Frida had painted. No one had criticized her for making them, had they? Perhaps drawing my own face wasn't so shameful after all.

Yet, Frida's paintings scared me. They were filled with symbols of pain and suffering that I couldn't grasp. Why were her paintings like that?

For my 26th birthday (my first birthday in the USA), my husband, Tim, gave me as a present the book *Frida Kahlo in Mexico* by Robin Richmond. This was the first book I read about Frida Kahlo, and I was immediately fascinated not only by her life, but also by the way she carried her Mexican identity with pride, wearing those peasant dresses that many people in Mexico don't want to wear because they are seen as symbols of low class. And then her artwork! Little by little I began to feel the heart beating in her paintings, the open veins, the broken back.

To my surprise I also began to learn that Frida was also a woman of laughs, jokes, and *palabrotas*. Her passion was also voiced in her search for justice in her political ideas. The more I learned about her the more that she became to me a beacon of creativity, and I knew that one day I would create a book about her. Like Frida, I wanted to create my own life as a work of art. And I had the tools to do it; we all do. We use them as we search, see, play, know, dream, feel, love… we can all create. We live. ¡Viva la vida!

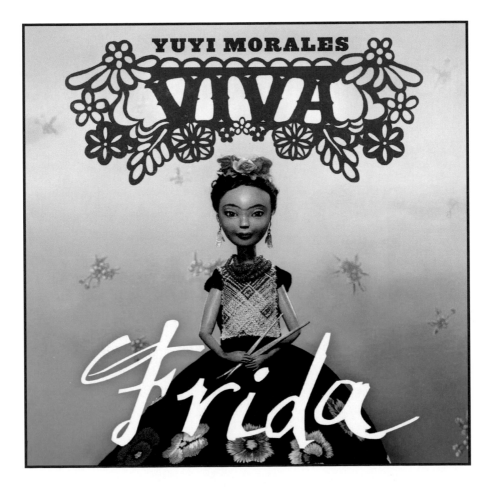

2015 Honor Book for Narrative

Portraits of Hispanic American Heroes
Juan Felipe Herrera

I had so many drafts of *Portraits of Hispanic American Heroes* that I could not slip out of my studio. But none made sense. They lacked a particular soul rhythm, even after carving out research from dusty books and articles and conducting mind-blowing interviews. I gave up—just couldn't get the stories right. My partner, Margarita, was with me; my agent, Kendra Marcus, and editor, Lucia Monfried, stood strong. Getting there—then, I noticed Raúl Colón's portrait of Joan Baez. There it is—in her loving eyes. Now it is here. Gracias, Pura Belpré Author Honor Award Committee—mil gracias!

2015 Honor Books for Illustration

Green Is a Chile Pepper
John Parra

There is such a special significance and emotion when winning a Pura Belpré Honor Award. It is a connection directly linked to your Latin heart, filled with family, friends, music, food, art, books, and culture. It knows that your hard work has been recognized for something that you have believed in and dedicated yourself to. It is also lots of fun! I was thrilled to receive my second recognition for my art illustrations in the book *Green Is a Chile Pepper*. Once again it is a privilege to be part of such an exclusive choice event.

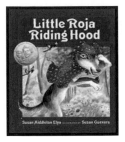

Little Roja Riding Hood
Susan Guevara

Everything is possible in the world of my heart and mind. I listen from there when I make art, and materials speak. Where I walk, the landscape speaks. The insensate animates and becomes a teacher. This is the world that I drew for *Little Roja*. It is also the northern New Mexico landscape where I live. The beauty here gives me courage and teaches me that we are beauty. We are part of the whole. Yet, all that is our history, our life situation, even our DNA, comes forward in a distinct, individual voice when we work from this truth.

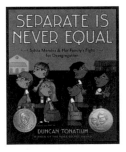

Separate Is Never Equal: Sylvia Mendez & Her Family's Fight for Desegregation
Duncan Tonatiuh

Mendez v. Westminster is a very important piece of American history that not many people know about. The case truly paved the way for the desegregation of schools across the United States. Unfortunately, a lot of inequality still exists. According to a 2012 study by the Civil Rights Project at UCLA, 43% of Latino students and 38% of black students attend schools where fewer than 10% of their classmates are white. Latino and black children are twice as likely to be in a school where the majority of students are poor. Therefore, their schools are likely to have fewer resources and less experienced teachers. The Mendez fight for justice is as relevant today as it was 70 years ago.

2014 Narrative Medal Winner

Meg Medina

Yaqui Delgado Wants to Kick Your Ass

I was raised in this country as a bicultural child, my parents having arrived from Cuba in the early 1960s. So, the fact that I write stories from a Latino child's perspective isn't so surprising.

But when I think of why it matters that I create this work, I think about the children who are sitting in classrooms today at a time when so few culturally diverse books are being published. Without books like the Pura Belpré selections, I worry that we offer only superficial stories about Latino foods and holidays or, at worst, stereotypes. I write about Latino families, then, so that readers can see their lives as they are—a rich, complicated, and beautiful part of the American tapestry.

When I wrote *Yaqui Delgado Wants to Kick Your Ass*, I began as I almost always do, from a place of memory. I had tangled with my own bullying in the seventh grade, an experience that gutted me.

But the truth is that I wasn't only writing the story of bullying. Instead, I was exploring how young Latinas find their voice and sense of self. I let Piddy flail through all of the questions I once had: Was I really Latina if I had been born here? If I had never been to Cuba? Did it matter that I spoke English better than Spanish? That I had no accent? Was it a blessing or a curse that I didn't look like the physical stereotype of Latinos? And most important of all, could my family and I really connect across all the ways in which we were different?

In the end, I gave Piddy the best ammunition a child can have in the tough business of growing up. I drew her world full of the strong women I remember as a child. I gave her the businesswoman and the minimum wage laborer. I gave her the sexually liberated and the morally bound Latina. I gave her confidantes and oppressors. I drew the women who had been dealt a lousy hand and learned how to play it anyway.

In short, I drew a complicated girl who was loved and protected more than she realized. I think readers of all ethnicities connect with Piddy's journey, but for Latino children in particular, I think they connect with what she had to fight to find out about herself.

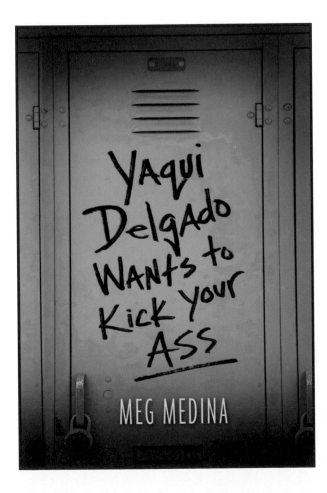

2014 Illustration Medal Winner

Yuyi Morales

Niño Wrestles the World

I am a mother of a *niño*. He and I came together to the USA when he was only a little baby. As a young child my son constantly challenged me with his curiosity about the world, with his resilient pursuit to learn, to read about, and to live those things that he loved, and also with his tenderness. As he grew up and accompanied me through my journey as an immigrant mother, he became my inspiration and my hero. I have learned much from my niño.

When I was a little child myself, one day my father took me and my little sisters to see *las luchas*. My father had practiced Olympic wrestling during his *juventud* and has always been a fan of sports in general. In addition, a friend of his was wrestling in the lucha show of the evening. My mother frowned. Lucha spectacles, she argued, were about people fighting, and she didn't want us, niñas, to get this idea that it was OK to fight. We went to las luchas regardless, and my father made sure that we didn't leave the place without meeting his *luchador* friend. What I remember is that he looked enormous, that his hands were huge and wrapped my fingers like carnitas when he shook my tiny hand.

When I decided I wanted to create a book about *lucha libre*, I went back to that evening at the luchas with my father. I have been reflecting much about the idea of how we all are *luchadores* with challenges that confront us in our daily lives, and how we wrestle them with the best that we know how. I wanted to create a book that honored children like my son, who had constantly gone through the world with a fiery passion for life, but I also wanted to honor the teachings of my mother, who believed that fighting should not be done to harm another, but to be the best that you can be. And what are children really, really good at? Children are experts at imagining, at playing, at making friends, at being awesome, aren't they? They have the most precious skills to wrestle the world.

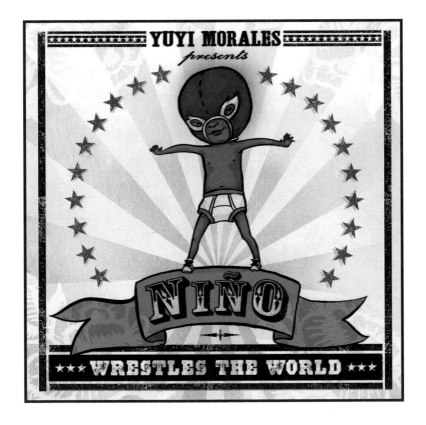

2014 Honor Books for Narrative

The Lightning Dreamer: Cuba's Greatest Abolitionist
Margarita Engle

I was thrilled to receive a Pura Belpré Honor for *The Lightning Dreamer*, a book that honors the great abolitionist and feminist writer Gertrudis Gómez de Avellaneda. Inspired by her courage to think independently and challenge the rules of her era, I wrote this book hoping that she would finally be recognized for her groundbreaking interracial romance novel, *Sab*, as well as her breathtaking poetry. I also hoped that her life story would help young readers think about their own decisions in creative ways.

The Living
Matt de la Peña

I'm not exaggerating at all when I say that winning the Pura Belpré Honor for my young adult novel *The Living* was a dream come true. I set out to write a commercial novel (featuring a Mexican American protagonist) that also reached for literary quality. I love the four quieter books I wrote before *The Living*, but I wanted to try something bigger, something outside my comfort zone. I'll admit, I was nervous. But then I got the call from the Belpré committee. I don't think I can adequately explain what this honor has meant to me.

Pancho Rabbit and the Coyote: A Migrant's Tale
Duncan Tonatiuh

According to a 2011 Pew Hispanic Center report, there are an estimated 1.5 million undocumented children in the U.S., and about 5.5 million children of undocumented immigrants in U.S. schools. Each year, men, women, and children go through extremely dangerous and often deadly journeys to reach this country. Yet of the thousands of books for children that are published every year, only a handful of them talk about this issue.

2014 Honor Books for Illustration

Maria Had a Little Llama/María tenía una Llamita
Angela Dominguez

The Pura Belpré Honor meant to me that a jury from my own community singled out my work as being notable both culturally and aesthetically. It also was, more plainly, the ultimate confidence booster. Especially since *Maria Had a Little Llama* began as an assignment for a SCBWI conference that I hoped would simply get me work as an illustrator. I just wanted to personalize the classic nursery rhyme with my love of Peruvian culture, through a fun, music-loving little girl and her llama. The fact that Henry Holt published it, and it received such a prestigious honor, continues to amaze me. *¡Gracias!*

Pancho Rabbit and the Coyote: A Migrant's Tale
Duncan Tonatiuh

I thought it was important to write and illustrate a book on the topic of undocumented immigrants. Children need to see themselves and their experiences in the books they read. It lets them know that their voices are important. For children who are not familiar with the undocumented experience, books about the topic can help create empathy and understanding.

Tito Puente: Mambo King/Rey del Mambo
Rafael López

I had the great honor to create a Tito Puente Latin Music Legend Stamp for the United States Postal Service. I poured over old videos of his exhilarating performances, scanned photos, and immersed myself fully into his music. What a thrill it was to again share the story of his genius and talent in a picture book just for children. The encouragement and support of Reforma and ALSC has made such a difference in my career and life. It has given me the chance to travel around the country connecting with amazing children, teachers, and librarians. Promoting reading and literacy with art has become my life's work, and I feel like I'm just warming up.

2013 Narrative Medal Winner

Benjamín Alire Sáenz

Aristotle and Dante Discover the Secrets of the Universe

Writing about the Latino experience? Simply put, it's the only thing I really know how to do. I write out of a physical, emotional, linguistic, psychological, and cultural landscape that, for me, is the American experience.

I grew up 42 miles from the U.S.-Mexico border. I grew up poor. I grew up speaking two languages. I grew up never quite feeling American and never quite feeling Mexican. I was neither and I was both. I cannot imagine having only one language living inside me just as I cannot imagine having grown up as part of the dominant culture—whatever the dominant culture is.

When I started writing, I wanted to be considered an "American writer." In truth, I have always been an American writer. It's just that the piece of America I wrote about and the Americans I wrote about weren't really recognized as being American. That has been a great burden in my life, and yet overcoming the obstacle of shouting "We are here! We are you!" actually helped me become the writer I am today. A writer must overcome obstacles, face the world, and write what he knows without apology but also with great humanity.

I stopped shouting and just wrote about the culture and the people I knew. But this is important: I do not perform my own ethnicity. Which is to say, that I do not write what I think the greater culture expects me to write. I do not turn my characters into cultural clichés and I do not write to inform—although I do inform. I let my readers in on the lives of the people who inhabit my cultural space, and I allow them to experience them as people. We are all just people.

It has been my great privilege to write about the people who have given me my voice. It has been my great privilege to write about the people who have helped make this country great. It has been and remains my great privilege to remind myself and my readers that difference and diversity matter—but more than that, that our common humanity and compassion binds us together.

2013 Illustration Medal Winner

David Díaz

Martín de Porres
The Rose in the Desert

The humble and extraordinary life of Martín de Porres was a radical departure in my work from the topics I had researched and illustrated in the previous three years, and one that I was very happy to embrace. As I read about the hardships of his childhood and the effort his mother made to place him under the care of the church, this character became endearing to me. I knew I wanted to portray his inner beauty, and I adjusted my style to bring to the forefront of the story the softness of his care for humanity and any other type of living creature.

Although the span of his life evolved until his death at the age of 59, my portraits of him showed a continuum of the same innocence and beauty he offered the world through his generosity and commitment to make this a better world for the poor and the sick.

It is widely accepted that he had a special virtue to communicate with animals, and that I thought would be one of the key elements of how young readers would think of Martín de Porres. Editors agreed with that vision, and it finally became the cover of the book.

The city of Lima in Perú was a prosperous and beautiful urban enclave in the sixteenth century. Many churches and cathedrals were built echoing those of Spain. I studied maps and reproduced the architectural style of gothic interiors that were present in that city at the time of Martín's life.

It was a great honor to receive the Pura Belpré Award for illustration in 2013 for *Martín de Porres: The Rose in the Desert*.

2013 Honor Book for Narrative

The Revolution of Evelyn Serrano
Sonia Manzano

As a Nuyorican raised in the South Bronx I knew little of the Puerto Rico my parents came from. Not seeing myself reflected in the society of the mid-1950s only added to my sense of lacking identity. I remember, however, coming across Belpré's stories of *Juan Bobo* and *Pérez y Martina* and feeling that those stories had something to do with the culture I subconsciously missed. All those thoughts and memories came back to me when my book *The Revolution of Evelyn Serrano* received the Pura Belpré Honor. Wouldn't it be wonderful if my books can do for others what Pura Belpré's books did for me?

No honor books for illustration were selected for 2013.

Portrait of Pura Belpré
Eric Velásquez, 2011

2012 Narrative Medal Winner

Guadalupe García McCall

Under the Mesquite

To be able to write the Latino cultural experience is very rewarding because it allows me to showcase the beauty of our traditions, illustrate what is in our hearts, give us voice, express our concerns, illustrate our struggles and fears, and highlight our hopes and dreams. In a way, by writing about the Latino cultural experience, I am hoping to shed a bit of light on the social and political issues affecting our culture and help others realize that, deep down inside, we are not any different than the rest of the world. We are humans. We are part of the blend of the beautiful fabric of our tiny corner of the universe.

There are a great many social conflicts and injustices still at play in the world in which we live, and I think communication and empathy are vital to the nature of resolution. However, there is more to resolution than tolerance, more than even acceptance—there is the need for true understanding and appreciation. If people don't know who we are, where we are coming from, why we say the things we say and do the things we do, they will never be able to empathize with the social injustices that are affecting us as a community. Latinos are a large part of the American social structure, but, like other cultures, we have our own unique voice, nuanced by rich traditions and values based on our complex and vibrant histories.

Under the Mesquite is not just a Mexican immigrant child's story. It is a story of familial love, a story of the joys and sorrows of chasing the American dream, a story of courage and resilience in the face of tragedy and personal loss. It is Lupita's heart that is exposed in *Under the Mesquite*. Yes, her roots and heritage are strong within her, and it is that cultural strength that anchors Lupita when the storm hits. However, it is her humanity, her familial values, her perseverance, that fortify her, sustain her spirit, and eventually help her find herself as she moves forward with her dreams in the United States. Writing the Mexican-American cultural experience as honestly and authentically as possible was important for me because it didn't just allow me to celebrate my culture; it gave me an opportunity to share that which we consider most valuable, the warmth in our hearts.

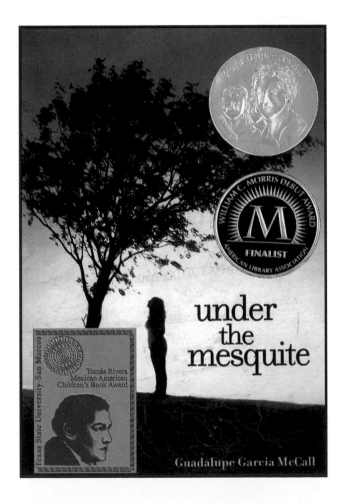

2012 Illustration Medal Winner

Duncan Tonatiuh

Diego Rivera
His World and Ours

I always draw my characters in profile and show their entire body. When I draw ears they look a little bit like the number three. My compositions are very geometric, and I tend to use a repetition of colors. It is an unusual way of drawing, but it comes from looking at the ancient art of the Americas, especially the Mixtec codex. I choose to draw like that in order to continue a tradition of art that was vibrant and existed for hundreds of years before the Europeans arrived.

In his murals and paintings Diego Rivera honored the art of the ancient Americans in a beautiful and exquisite way. Rivera was an avid Pre-Columbian art collector. He owned hundreds of sculptures made by Aztecs, Mayas, and other ancient cultures. The geometry, elegance, and monumentality of the sculptures he collected shines through in his artwork.

What I admire the most about Rivera is that he honored the past and was at the same time able to make images that were relevant to the people that lived in his day and age. His work is packed with poignant social and political commentary. I aspire to do something similar with my work. I hope my illustrations inspire young readers today to learn about the art from the past, but I also hope that the artwork feels relevant and relatable to their world and experiences.

Rivera tackled all the major historical events of Mexico in his work: the conquest, the independence, and the revolution. He also made murals about major advances in science and technology that occurred in the first half of the twentieth century, like the assembly line and the use of atomic energy. His murals are luminous and epic. I have had a chance to see many of them. While looking at Rivera's work I began to wonder what he would paint nowadays. Would he paint satellites? Bluetooth? People using laptops and smartphones? That thought was the initial spark behind *Diego Rivera: His World and Ours*.

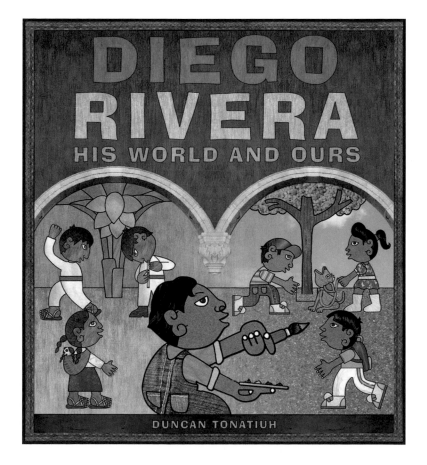

2012 Honor Books for Narrative

Hurricane Dancers:
The First Caribbean Pirate Shipwreck
Margarita Engle

When my most complex verse novel received a Pura Belpré Honor, I was overjoyed. *Hurricane Dancers* is an exploration of the first encounter between violent Spanish conquistadors and the indigenous Cubans of the south-central coast, where my own maternal Ciboney Taíno ancestors have lived for thousands of years.

I chose to tell this story in the voice of a mestizo boy for whom the culture clash is personal. Writing this book was a way for me to rediscover the mysteries Quebrado explores after a hurricane frees him from the pirate ship.

I hope that young readers will be able to read *Hurricane Dancers* as a survival tale, while older readers might find additional layers: a love story, the riddles of history, and an homage to peacekeepers.

Maximilian and the Mystery of the Guardian Angel:
A Bilingual Lucha Libre Thriller
Xavier Garza

To receive a Pura Belpré Honor Book Award for *Maximilian and the Mystery of the Guardian Angel* was truly an incredible experience for me, especially because it was a book that portrayed something that I hold dear to my heart… *lucha libre*!

I am a big believer in celebrating both our Latino culture and heritage. I believe that both our written stories and our art give us our very identity as a people. So to receive an award that celebrates that very culture and identity tugs at my heartstrings. I was both humbled and honored at the same time.

The Cazuela That the Farm Maiden Stirred
Rafael López

This adventure was based on a familiar story—the house that Jack built—but was told in a new way. With the book's purposeful, repetitive nature, I was challenged to keep it lively and compelling, so it meant a great deal that Reforma and ALSC acknowledged my efforts. For me, color is an expression of my identity and my heritage, and I believe it is the most direct route to the emotions of children and families who will turn the pages of my books. It's reassuring to know the hues and subtle textures I scraped, dabbed, and coaxed into life resonated to put a twist on this well-known tale.

Marisol McDonald Doesn't Match/
Marisol McDonald no combina
Sara Palacios

Winning such a prestigious award like the Pura Belpré has a special meaning to me. Being an immigrant myself I was honored to be able to bring to life through my illustrations, a character so diverse as Marisol McDonald, who represents so many children growing up in the U.S. today. It is my hope that this story will bring awareness to the fact that being different and embracing each other's unique qualities is the first step in becoming a more inclusive society, free of prejudices, and that our cultural backgrounds, whatever they are, can only enrich us as human beings.

Pam Muñoz Ryan

The Dreamer

I received the medal for *The Dreamer* at the Pura Belpré's "Quinces." The Pura Belpré Award had come of age!

My book *The Dreamer* was a story about coming of age, too. It is about a boy, Neftalí Reyes, who was painfully shy but often felt there was something yet to be discovered about himself, something at his core that might validate his being. He found that *something* in his writing and grew up to be the poet Pablo Neruda.

I often reminisce with my sister and cousins about our grandmother, Esperanza, and how she used to embarrass us with her pride. If she had any one of us with her and she stopped to talk to someone, she'd nudge us forward and say, "This is my granddaughter. Isn't she beautiful?" Oh, how we wanted to crawl into a hole!

Once, when I was an acne-ridden adolescent who had not yet grown into my nose or my feet, I was with my grandmother at Mr. Louey's market, standing in front of the meat counter. She said, "Mr. Louey, this is my granddaughter. Isn't she beautiful?" Mr. Louey said nothing, handed her a roast wrapped in paper, smirked, and turned away. It was clear he did not see anything special in front of him. I had been dismissed by the butcher.

I was paralyzed with embarrassment. My grandmother grabbed my hand, pulled me away, and, in the way she sometimes translated Spanish to English, said, "Do not worry. He does not see the bones of you."

Then, I remember thinking that my grandmother was ridiculous and infuriating. Now, I know she meant that he could not see my core, the essence of me, the potential in me.

I cannot help but feel that the Pura Belpré committee and the luminous medal are like my proud grandmother—a persistent compliment. The award nudges the book forward. It suggests that the literary community pay attention to the Latino experience. It points out that there is something special that should not be dismissed. It promises that someone might see the bones of us.

2011 Illustration Medal Winner

Eric Velásquez

Grandma's Gift

As an Afro-Latino author/illustrator, creating literary works for children sometimes could be a daunting task. It is as though the world has created labeled boxes for everyone to fit into, but the label for your box has conspicuously gone missing. The strangest part of this scenario is that everyone in a labeled box is constantly telling you that you do not belong in his or her box. Fortunately, my grandmother prepared me for this challenge in life.

I come from a proud Afro-Latino family that can trace its roots in Puerto Rico to before the 1860s, which is to say, as far back as the census records go back (at least for now). "You come from a long line of educated and talented people," my grandmother would always say to me. Her comforting words have guided me for many years.

My grandmother was the inspiration for *Grandma's Gift,* the book that won the 2011 Pura Belpré Award for illustration. My grandmother shared a great many stories, music, theories, and recipes with me. Ultimately, what compelled me most to write and illustrate *Grandma's Gift* is the fact that there are so few books featuring images of Afro-Latinos.

Soon after I won the award I was asked to paint a portrait of Pura Belpré for the cover of the 2011 award ceremony program guide. While researching images of Pura Belpré I was astounded to discover that she lived in Santurce, Puerto Rico, which is where my grandmother was from, and they both had attended Central High School. Upon reading Pura Belpré's biography I discovered that she was born in the year 1899, compared to my grandmother being born in 1909. The possibility of these two women passing each other on the streets of Santurce or sharing casual conversation at the market square was completely plausible.

But the most amazing part of doing the research was looking through hundreds of photographs of Pura Belpré and thinking how she might even be related to my grandma because of her beautiful familiar features and stylish disposition. Suddenly I felt so proud, knowing that I could claim Pura Belpré as one of my people. Her many accomplishments and love of literacy and storytelling were so much like my grandmother and her stories of the people of Santurce, Puerto Rico. I felt so overwhelmed with the notion that my unlabeled box was never a box after all, but more like a nation of people. The people of African descent who love storytelling, literature, art, and music, people who have sacrificed so much of themselves because of their belief in the future.

Thinking back to 2011, I feel as though I won more than one award. Because of the marvelous awakening in me, I like to call it "Pura's Gift."

2011 Honor Books for Narrative

The Firefly Letters: A Suffragette's Journey to Cuba
Margarita Engle

When Fredrika Bremer, a Swedish suffragist, traveled to Cuba in 1851, she left the most complete known record of daily life on the island at that time. Her journals and letters revealed aspects of the lives of women, and slaves, that could not be openly discussed by Cuban writers, who were limited by censorship. I was fascinated by her role as an outsider, and by her friendship with Cecilia, a young slave assigned as her translator. Together, they wandered the countryside, rescuing captive fireflies, and interviewing captive people. I am grateful for the Pura Belpré Honor received by this simple story of hope.

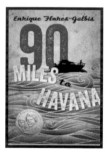

90 Miles to Havana
Enrique Flores-Galbis

I wrote *90 Miles to Havana* to tell the story of how my brothers and I arrived in the U.S. This story is intertwined with the complex history of "Operation Pedro Pan," the largest exodus of unaccompanied children in the history of the western hemisphere. The Pura Belpré Honor Award empowered this story and swept it before a larger audience, ensuring that it would endure in the stream of dialogue about this historic moment. I'm thankful and proud that *90 Miles to Havana* has found its place in the sea of immigrant tales that help shape the American narrative.

¡Olé! Flamenco
George Ancona

As a teenager I began to take classic guitar lessons. But once I saw and heard flamenco music and dance I switched. Soon I was able to pay for flamenco dance classes. But by then I had quit my job as an art director to become a freelance photographer. I began to travel on assignments and was unable to practice, and the guitar is still in the closet. Doing the book allowed me to travel to Sevilla and plunge into the flamenco world. After all, a guy's got to make a living.

2011 Honor Books for Illustration

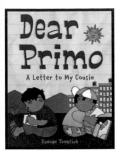

Dear Primo: A Letter to My Cousin
Duncan Tonatiuh

I grew up in Mexico and came to the U.S. as a teenager. For some years I lived in a neighborhood in Brooklyn with a large Mexican enclave. The thing that struck me the most when I moved there were the children. They looked just like the kids that I grew up with, but they were in a totally different environment. They played, however, with the same enthusiasm that my friends and I did when we were kids. The thing I have learned by living in two countries is that despite the apparent differences—the buildings, the language, the food—at the end of the day we are more alike than different. I hope that *Dear Primo* delivers that message.

Fiesta Babies
Amy Córdova

I had so much fun imagining and inventing the toddlers who frolic through *Fiesta Babies*. Each one seemed to develop his or her individual personality as I painted. Fiesta in our part of the country is a beloved family and community event, filled with grand excitement, pageantry, and the colorful honoring of multicultural traditions. My artistic intent was to capture the joy and energy of little ones in the midst of celebration and to depict the tender love of family and friends. Receiving my second Pura Belpré Honor for the illustration of *Fiesta Babies* evokes my deepest happiness and gratitude. This cherished award completely affirmed my every intention in creating the artwork.

Me, Frida
David Díaz

Having worked on the life of Diego Rivera the year before I started on Frida's biography meant that I lived those days surrounded by books and paintings by and about this famous couple. However, the author Amy Novesky centered her writing on a moment of Frida's life, her arrival to San Francisco, and her sense of wonder and loss, new encounters, and discovery of self. This required a concentrated effort to illustrate emotions as well as situations, a challenge I enjoyed on every page.

2010 Narrative Medal Winner

Julia Álvarez

Return to Sender

In 1960, my family arrived in New York City from the Dominican Republic, fleeing the dictatorship of Trujillo. I was ten years old, but I had never set foot in a library. It turns out that dictators don't approve of places that open up people's minds and free their imaginations.

Of course, it takes more than a building to make a library. You need librarians, curators of this treasure, who make you feel at home in the United States of the Imagination where all books reside. That's where I really landed in 1960, the homeland of the imagination, and one of the ways to get there is by going to the library.

If it hadn't been for librarians welcoming me to this grand world of stories, I never would have become a reader, much less a writer.

Even so, as a young immigrant and new reader in a second language, I never thought that one day I would be on those shelves.

The Pura Belpré Award for *Return to Sender* came as a vote of confidence during a critical moment in our country's history: Draconian laws and ordinances, raids and deportations, including the dragnet operation in 2006 that gives the novel its name. This is truly the ongoing civil rights struggle of our times and, obviously, a highly charged personal issue for me.

As with most of my books, I didn't set out to write about this topic. It found me. I live in what I call the Latino-compromised state of Vermont, the state with the smallest Latino population. But in the last fifteen years we've seen a huge influx of Mexican migrant workers on Vermont dairy farms, many of them undocumented. Their kids have begun showing up in our local schools. Because I'm one of the few Spanish speakers in my county, I'm often asked to translate for them and to talk to the Vermont kids about Latino cultures and customs. When I first began volunteering, I found a troubled, anxious group of kids. The Vermont kids didn't understand why their farmer parents told them to keep those workers a secret. The Mexican and Mexican-American kids lived in fear that their parents would be taken away. I thought we all need a story to understand what is happening to us.

The Pura Belpré Award recognizes that we need stories to understand what is happening to us as a nation. Once again librarians have welcomed me to the bookshelves of American literature. From the bottom of my heart and *mi corazón*, thank you and *gracias*.

2010 Illustration Medal Winner

Rafael López

Book Fiesta!
*Celebrate Children's Day/Book Day
Celebremos El día de los niños/
El día de los libros*

Receiving the Pura Belpré Medal for *Book Fiesta* was the gift of a lifetime. A thrilling, pivotal moment in my career that reinforced both my work as an artist and a lifelong passion for books.

Growing up in Mexico City, my father would take me to the Lagunilla flea market where we would get lost in the magic of collecting books other people left behind. I also regularly traveled over an hour by *metro* in my quest to get to the Hemeroteca, our central library. More than words, I discovered fascinating and exotic images, treasures from all over the world that awakened my curiosity for life. The stacks of books were my playground. I learned that when you read, your imagination has no boundaries.

The message of Pat Mora's book is simple and powerful: READ! As I created the illustrations for this story, I wanted kids to fall head over heels for books. When you believe in an idea, like I did in this one, you can't wait to grab your paintbrushes and share that excitement with children by inviting the sun and the moon to the book party. Books teach us that the world we live in is such a wonderfully diverse place. I strive to show this in my characters, creating scenes that focus on giving each child a distinctive personality. When reading, children often dream they are the heroes of fantastic stories, and I was determined to convey that spirit of magic and transformation.

My mother flew for the first time from Mexico to Washington, D.C., in order to attend the 2010 Pura Belpré ceremony. I will never forget the look on her face. She taught me to believe in my dreams of becoming an artist. I realized how important it is to communicate that vital message to all children. This recognition opened so many doors for me, making it possible to make a living creating diverse books. My thanks goes out to librarians, teachers, parents, and volunteers who day in and day out turn the pages of books and help make the words and pictures come to life.

2010 Honor Books for Narrative

Diego: Bigger Than Life
Carmen T. Bernier-Grand

After my research for *Frida: ¡Viva la vida! Long Live Life!* I decided that a biography of Diego Rivera had to follow. He appealed to me because, like me, he was a storyteller. In his hometown of Guanajuato, Mexico, I saw that, at his birth, he really wasn't dumped in a dung bucket as he used to say. Instead, he had a comfortable crib that rocked. All his life, he called for attention. On the other hand, his magnificent murals called for the attention of those who suffered. Who was this man? I had to find out.

Frederico García Lorca
Georgina Lázaro

Winning the Pura Belpré Honor for the book *Federico García Lorca* was a very happy and significant event. The award is named after a Puerto Rican woman, like me, and the first Latina librarian at the New York Public Library. Winning the award was a way of bringing her name back to our island, which meant a lot to me and to our people. This recognition was awarded to a book conceived in Puerto Rico and written in Spanish, which made us all feel a sense of pride in our heritage and our culture, as well as being proud of the beauty, the music, and the magic of our language.

2010 Honor Books for Illustration

Diego: Bigger Than Life
David Díaz

The memory of working on a biographical account of a famous Latino character was still fresh in my mind when I received the request to illustrate the life of Diego Rivera. But this time it was even closer to my heart as Diego was the big light in the sky of artists that I admire. The genre employed by the author, Carmen T. Bernier-Grand, were poems that stand alone but relate to one another telling the life of Rivera. These poems helped me to envision moments of his life, one that I wanted to portray with the glamour and beauty of his splendid art.

Gracias · Thanks
John Parra

Receiving the Pura Belpré Honor for Illustration for my book *Gracias · Thanks* was an incredible experience that was completely new to me. It introduced me to the wonderful and expanded world of librarians, educators, and book lovers. The award event itself was a celebration of amazing Latino literature and art. It was in this shared community I felt a spirited and passionate connection for the education, culture, and family experience that is Pura Belpré.

My Abuelita
Yuyi Morales

Sometimes people ask me about my favorite art technique, and I tell them that all art-making is my favorite since it is all new to me, for I began making art when I was already an adult. For *My Abuelita*, I wanted to do something I always loved when I was a child. I wanted to play with my dolls. I was scared, because I didn't know how I was going to create a book like this, but when my husband Tim and I were at the studio setting the scenes to be photographed, I felt exactly like little playful Yuyi—and it was perfect.

2009 Narrative Medal Winner

Margarita Engle

The Surrender Tree
Poems of Cuba's Struggle for Freedom

The story of Rosa, la bayamesa, fascinated me for many reasons. As a botanist, I was intrigued by her use of wild plants as medicine. As a Cuban-American, I longed to know more about the history of my mother's homeland. As a writer, I was eager to take on the challenge of an honest portrayal of Cuba's three wars for independence from Spain.

I wrote *The Surrender Tree* with the hope that young readers would feel inspired to write their own poetry. I also wanted to show them that no matter how impossible a situation seems, kindness and courage can change the world. It is primarily a story of the hope for peace, not a story about battles.

The result was astonishing. Even though *The Surrender Tree* was poetry, a form often ignored by award committees, it received both the Pura Belpré Medal and the first Newbery Honor ever awarded to a Latino author.

I felt a sense of disbelief. How could this be the first Latino Newbery Honor, when so many giants had written before me? Was it simply a matter of timing? Yes, it was timing, and it was also the result of visibility granted to authors who receive awards such as the Pura Belpré, which allow us to keep publishing, and to keep having our new books reviewed. Without that visibility, we would sink into the enormous mass of volumes published each year.

One of the happiest outcomes of the visibility gained by *The Surrender Tree* was a dual language paperback. One of my goals is to write books that can be used by family literacy projects, with several generations reading and discussing the same story, or in the case of poetry, even one small portion of a story. Without the Pura Belpré Medal and Newbery Honor, *The Surrender Tree* would have ended its print run without a translation. With these awards, a unique bilingual edition was possible.

De músico, poeta, y loco
todos tenemos un poco
Of musician, poet, and lunatic
we all have a little bit

The Pura Belpré Committee understood this folk saying, and honored the crazy poet who wrote a book expecting so little, and receiving so much. By doing so, they also honored the tradition of verse in Latin America, where poetry is a part of daily life. I will forever be indebted to their vision of a future linked to the past.

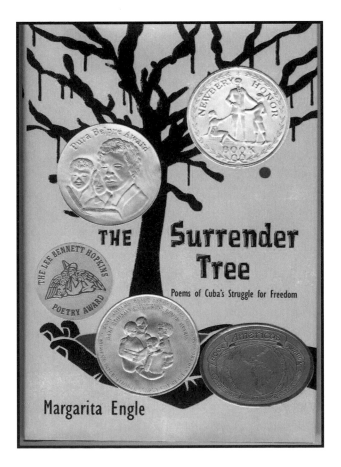

Yuyi Morales

Just in Case
A Trickster Tale
and Spanish Alphabet Book

After having written and illustrated *Just a Minute: A Trickster Tale and Counting Book*, I sometimes fantasized what another book featuring the misadventures of the skeleton *Señor Calavera* could be about. I had created *Just a Minute* during an evening class where our teacher had instructed us to come up with a story to illustrate in the format of a concept book. At the time I had chosen to make a counting book, but...what to count? I have always been fascinated by the folk stories from Mexico, especially the trickster tales in which powerful beings, such as death or the devil, are defeated by common people such as you and me. And from that inspiration, the story of Grandma Beetle tricking Señor Calavera was born.

But I had also decided that the story of *Just a Minute* was going to be a single book, and for a long while I put my idea of a sequel behind, until one day while visiting the city of Veracruz with my husband Tim. Veracruz is the city where Tim and I had met and in which our son, Kelly, had been born. It is also the sultry place we left behind when we emigrated to the U.S. Walking by the seawall I began telling Tim how I sometimes wondered what a new book about Señor Calavera could be about. It would be another concept book, I told him, perhaps this time an alphabet book. And, didn't Señor Calavera promise Grandma Beetle that he would come back for her next birthday party, anyway? One thing was clear about Señor Calavera, I told Tim, given his very nature, he surely knew nothing about celebrating life and birthdays. Señor Calavera wouldn't know anything about presents! Maybe he could learn the art of giving by finding a present for each letter of the alphabet.

It was during that conversation, in front of the the sea of Veracruz, when I realized that I would love to make what eventually became *Just in Case: A Trickster Tale and Spanish Alphabet Book*.

On my flight back home to California I created a list of my favorite words from every letter of the Spanish alphabet, and in the process, I realized how many awesome presents I could give simply with the letter *CH!*

2009 Honor Books for Narrative

Just in Case: A Trickster Tale and Spanish Alphabet Book
Yuyi Morales

In 2009 I received double good news. *Just in Case* had also received a Pura Belpré Honor for the narrative! Writing the story of *Señor Calavera* trying to find a present for Grandma Beetle had been my own declaration of love to the Spanish language. The narrative intertwined the Spanish alphabet with a story of friendship and the care that one can take to find the right present for a loved one. It is also a trickster tale, which means that the reader could be tricked as well. Look again! Things might not be what they appear to be at first.

Reaching Out
Francisco Jiménez

It is essential for Latino children and young adults to see themselves in literature—and for all children and young adults to read about all the diverse cultures that are an integral part of American history. If we are to understand better who we are as a nation, we must learn about the experiences of all different peoples, break down barriers that separate us, and see ourselves reflected in the other. I wrote *Reaching Out* to describe the experiences of many students, especially Latinos who, like me, are the first in their families to attend college, as well as to pay tribute to teachers who help their students be responsive to social and civic obligations in an ever-changing world.

The Storyteller's Candle/ La velita de los cuentos
Lucía González

I wrote *The Storyteller's Candle/ La velita de los cuentos* as an homage to Pura Belpré, inspired by the work of the visionary children's librarian, who was a pioneer in providing services to immigrant families and who understood the importance of honoring the immigrants' languages and preserving their stories. The main characters in the story, Hildamar and Santiago's feelings and the family's nostalgia for the homeland, reflect my own immigrant experience.

2009 Honor Books for Illustration

Papá and Me
Rudy Gutiérrez

Art for me means humbly translating the magic that surrounds me into visuals, with the idea that it can be a tool to educate, medicine to heal the soul's wounds, and a bridge that connects one soul to another. My work is my life. Something that allows me to realize my own value by inspiring others to see their own "divinity." As a Latino of Puerto Rican descent, the reality is that we don't see enough images that represent our special "magic." I am thankful to be acknowledged for my efforts in working toward honoring this responsibility that accompanies the act of making art!

The Storyteller's Candle/ La velita de los cuentos
Lulu Delacre

Fluttering feathers / a rooster's song, / whirling colors wrapped in a bow. / Soft, gentle words, / a mother's joy, / tiny hands' dimples / toddlers' giggles. / A glowing candle, / the smell of books, / words transporting you, words that soothe.

These are the images that came to me when I was asked what it was like to have received this award. The Pura Belpré Honor is not the seal, nor the sale of books, but the knowledge that little hands of many colors will flip through the pages that reflect the faces they belong to. Faces that will laugh, or cry, or simply feel included and understood.

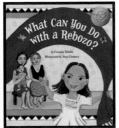

What Can You Do with a Rebozo?
Amy Córdova

As a descendant of New Mexican Natives with Hispanic ancestors, featuring Latino characters is always dear to my heart. Carmen Tafolla's rhyming style is simple, humorous, and appeals to young children. I love children, our cultural heritage, bright and saturated colors, so our collaboration was a perfect creative match! Receiving the call that my illustrations were selected as a Pura Belpré Honor came as a complete surprise, and one I wholeheartedly treasure. The award was a magnificent confirmation of my art, love of children, and commitment to the authentic visual telling of stories within our cultural context.

2008 Narrative Medal Winner

Margarita Engle

The Poet Slave of Cuba
A Biography of
Juan Francisco Manzano

My first book for young readers was an experiment. I had been writing prose for adults when I began researching the life of Juan Francisco Manzano. He taught himself to read and write while he was still a child, and still enslaved. His story seemed suited to the verse novel form. Since only the first half of his autobiographical notes survived nineteenth-century censorship, most of the known facts about his life are limited to his youth. I decided to try writing a book for young readers. It was a turning point in my career. I fell in love with the poetic form, and with the unique sense of connection to the future that a writer receives from communicating with young readers.

I wrote *The Poet Slave of Cuba* because I admired Manzano's courage, and I wrote it in verse because he was a poet. My hope was that modern children might learn from his passion for words. To Manzano, education was a great privilege. Books were also a comfort. Poetry was his secret doorway to freedom.

So many surprises came from this book! I discovered that many Americans were unaware of the existence of slavery in Latin America.

I learned that they cared about Cuban history, after half a century of hostilities between my parents' two countries. I also learned that the multiple voice format offered me complete freedom of expression. I could portray many attitudes, not just my own.

When *The Poet Slave of Cuba* received the Pura Belpré Award, I was stunned. Seeing Sean Qualls's beautiful cover art on the award poster was an incredible thrill. Holding the weight of the medal in my hand was amazing. Singing "De Colores" at the *Celebración* was emotional. I was not yet familiar enough with the world of children's literature to realize just how dramatically this award would impact my future. My next book could go directly to my wonderful editor, Reka Simonsen, instead of getting lost in a slush pile. The encouragement was immeasurable, and my gratitude is profound.

Yuyi Morales

Los Gatos Black on Halloween

From the very beginning I loved this bilingual Halloween story Marisa Montes created. There was such an irresistible playfulness not only to the story, but also to the way English and Spanish mingled to form spooky rich scenes.

In my first Halloween in the USA, I pushed my son's stroller through the suburban neighborhood where I lived with my husband's family. I gasped at the dark house's decorations and winced at the bloody toy chainsaws laying on the lawns. When I looked up at the trees, I found all kinds of hanging dead: ghosts, witches, evil-looking skeletons, and even figures and artifacts taken from horror movies. Halloween was meant to scare! I knew about being scared. During my childhood I had grown through the stories my aunts and uncles told about their encounters with anything from the weeping *Llorona* to little people called *chaneques*, who usually got children lost.

When I accepted the offer to illustrate Marisa's story I wondered if our publishers understood what they had gotten into when tasking a Latina to illustrate this book. I was ready to have a Halloween of my own style!

I am a fan of research, and I am a fan of stories. Putting together the menagerie of scary creatures that would haunt this book took me all the way to my own childhood in Mexico. My drawing table was invaded with stories and pictures of all kinds of dead people and other monsters I knew about. If you open the book, you will find them: witches riding their brooms in the style of X Games skateboarders and bicycle riders. The skeleton of Simón Bolívar, *el Libertador de América*, dances in a procession. *La Llorona*, the Weeping Woman, also makes an apparition. A mummy from Peru escapes his museum confinement. A nerdy wolf man carries his school report card in his pocket. The ghost of Mexican dictator Porfirio Díaz rises from his tomb. The ghost of *La Planchada*, the nurse with the well-ironed uniform who visits many Mexican hospitals, also makes her way to the monstrous ball. The dancing floor is taken by the ghost of the poet Sor Juana Inés de la Cruz, by an Olmec head, by Cantinflas, Diego Rivera, Tin Tan, Josefa Ortíz de Domínguez, an Aztec goddess called Cihuateteo, and even my aunts whom I always suspected to be witches.

In the pages of the book, my son lets me button his coat as we both come out of our coffins to join this Halloween monster's parade.

2008 Honor Books for Narrative

Frida ¡Viva la vida! Long Live Life!
Carmen T. Bernier-Grand

I wanted to write a biography about a woman and who better than Frida Kahlo? I had always been interested in artists, and Frida had such a life! One tragedy after another: At age six, she suffered from polio; at age eighteen, going home from school, her bus crashed into a trolley and a handrail impaled her through her pelvis. She had surgery after surgery and had to stay in bed a lot. Some people ask why Frida's paintings are so small. Well, how could a large canvas fit in bed? She asked her mother to place a mirror under the bed canopy so she could paint herself. What a woman! What an inspiration!

Los Gatos Black on Halloween
Marisa Montes (1951–2011)

Marisa Montes was very excited to be honored with the Pura Belpré Honor Award. She was exceedingly proud of her Puerto Rican heritage, including the folktales and other stories that she read and that were told to her by her family when she was growing up. She felt very strongly that these stories taught important lessons that still apply today, and that they were fun for both young readers and parents. She also felt that it is extremely important to preserve the Puerto Rican culture by learning the stories and speaking Spanish. She felt that receiving the Pura Belpré Honor Award validated these feelings and her pride in her culture.

Martina the Beautiful Cockroach: A Cuban Folktale
Carmen Agra Deedy

Every children's author I know writes with the cheerful hope that her book will be loved by young readers. That's why we do what we do. But to win the approbation of your peers provokes its own giddy feeling. When I learned that *Martina the Beautiful Cockroach* had won a Pura Belpré Honor Award, I did a Cuban-styled happy dance. Why? Because Pura Belpré—the award's titular Puerto Rican librarian and storyteller—perfectly represents the spirit of this most Latin award. That Latinos now have such an award is extraordinary. To receive one is cause for one uninhibited happy dance.

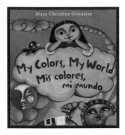

My Colors, My World/ Mis colores, mi mundo
Maya Christina González

As a queer Chicana, writing and illustrating my own children's book felt like an act of claiming self. The book's art shows how I found my reflection in nature (because I didn't find it in books growing up). I had a child's awareness of not belonging in the larger societal structure, but my father taught me through nature that I did belong. Receiving the award felt like belonging too. It placed me within the expanding spiral of Chicano/as affirming our sense of self and belonging, reconnecting us to our eternal creative power and ability to express and value our presence and perspective.

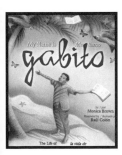

My Name Is Gabito: The Life of Gabriel García Márquez/
Me llamo Gabito: La vida de Gabriel García Márquez
Raúl Colón

When sketching ideas for *My Name Is Gabito*, nothing could be easier. Gabriel García Márquez could write such imaginative visuals that it could only inspire any visual artist to unleash his or her own versions of such imagery. There is no doubt that I benefitted from reading García Márquez's works, which in turn helped me illustrate the pieces you see in *Gabito*. The ideas flowed into my brain like an endless stream of cool, clear water on a hot day. The "heat" meant meeting the deadline, but the "cool water" meant everything flowed smoothly. I hope other young minds enjoy the visuals and Monica Brown's beautifully written book as much as I did in visualizing both, Gabo's and Monica's words.

2006 Narrative Medal Winner

Viola Canales

The Tequila Worm

My novel *The Tequila Worm*—that many find funny and full of festivity—was ironically inspired by the sudden and unexpected death of my father, which flipped my world upside down, causing me to feel my mortality for the very first time.

In conjuring up my most meaningful, treasured memories of my late father, I tapped into the rituals and celebrations that helped shape and weave our South Texas family and community together. Many traditions are deeply rooted in our culture, going back centuries, since my family, as many Mexican-American families still living in the Southwest, have been living there before there was even a United States or a Mexico.

The Tequila Worm enables readers to personally taste and experience the rich and deeply spiritual Mexican-American culture of South Texas by engaging with the main character Sofía, who learns the customs of her barrio—such as celebrating *quinceañeras* and the Day of the Dead, as well as making *cascarones* for Easter, and a *nacimiento* for Christmas. But when Sofía turns fifteen and leaves home to attend a boarding school over three hundred miles away that is Episcopalian, not Catholic, and for the well-off, not like those from her barrio, she steps into another world. Sofía, however, after struggling through the clash of the two different worlds, eventually learns to weave the two together, making an entirely new and empowering world for herself by grounding herself in the riches of her family's history and traditions that dispel the taunting and discrimination she encounters.

My personal Mexican-American culture—as is true for Sofía—the one I was raised in, continues to animate and inspire my writing to this day, whether prose or poetry, because, despite two degrees from Harvard University and having held several so-called important positions through the years, I'll never forget that it was a humble *curandera*, with little or no formal education, who finally cured me of a serious illness as a child, and with only one single chicken egg, where all the fancy, degreed doctors and specialists I had consulted before had failed.

Yes, I continue to dream and write about the Latino, Mexican-American culture because, for me, it is filled with the richest love, spirituality, and mystery, as well as the highest absurdities, craziness, and falling down laughter.

2006 Illustration Medal Winner

Raúl Colón

Doña Flor
A Tall Tale About a Giant Woman with a Great Big Heart

Drawing has long been a hunger that I have to satisfy. Therefore I draw.

But when I'm asked to illustrate a piece or a picture book involving Latino culture, there's an added incentive to pour my deepest thoughts and feelings into the work. It was appropriate and an honor to receive the award that has Pura Belpré's name attached to it.

The imagery that the written words of Pat Mora stirred in me greatly inspired the finished art for the book *Doña Flor*. It's fun when the mind goes crazy with shapes and colors and the hand can hardly keep up with it. My hope is that these collaborations lead to a better understanding of our Latino experience in America, as well as the culture of others.

About the book: Doña Flor is a giant lady who lives in a tiny village. Popular with her neighbors, she lets the children use her flowers as trumpets and her leftover tortillas as rafts. Flor loves to read, too, and she can often be found reading aloud to the children. One day, all the villagers hear a terrifying noise: it sounds like a huge animal bellowing just outside their village. Everyone is afraid, but not Flor. She wants to protect her beloved neighbors, so with the help of her animal friends, she sets off for the highest mesa to find the creature. Soon enough, though, the joke is on Flor and her friends, who come to rescue her, as she discovers the small secret behind that great big noise.

2006 Honor Books for Narrative

Becoming Naomi León
Pam Muñoz Ryan

In 1997, while reading an art book on woodcarving, I came across a reference to the Night of the Radishes, a festival where Oaxacan woodcarvers come to Oaxaca, Mexico, and sculpt scenes out of radishes. When I visited, I knew that I would someday use the magnificent festival in a book. In my story, the characters journey from California to Oaxaca City to find their father. During the writing, I examined my beginnings growing up half-Mexican and wondered what that might be like for children today. As always, I am grateful for the Pura Belpré recognition and the exposure it continues to bring to the diverse lives of my characters.

César: ¡Sí, se puede! Yes, We Can!
Carmen T. Bernier-Grand

Write a biography of César Chávez? I, a Puerto Rican who doesn't have a drop of Mexican blood? I, who has never lived in California? I, who doesn't even like to garden? I did stop eating grapes for *La Causa*, but I didn't march for it. How could I write about César Chávez? I studied every word I could find on César Chávez. I walked listening to Mexican music, ate Mexican food, talked to farm workers, farm owners, union leaders. Then it happened! César Chávez gripped my heart. It was time to write about him.

Doña Flor: A Tall Tale About a Giant Woman with a Great Big Heart
Pat Mora

We all need to know the names of the brave. I'm grateful to Latina librarians Oralia Garza de Cortés and Sandra Ríos Balderrama who introduced me (and us) to Pura Belpré, a giant woman with a great big heart.

2006 Honor Books for Illustration

Arrorró, mi niño: Latino Lullabies and Gentle Games
Lulu Delacre

Singing softly to myself *rimas y ritmos* from my childhood. Bells and giggles and sweet scent while I painted Latinas from many countries living in América. Our skin color is as varied as the places we call home. You might see us at the library, the art museum, or gently picking strawberries under a hot sun. The love for our children connects us. And in a *cancioncita* from *nuestros abuelos* we convey centuries of ingrained traditions that give our children roots. A gentle game, *un arrullo*, the beginning of the love of language in a mother's song.

César: ¡Sí, se puede! Yes, We Can!
David Díaz

The life of César Chávez has inspired all of us to commit to goals of justice and generosity. He was a man of principles who changed the letter of the law to correct the injustices suffered by farmworkers. I embraced this project by Carmen T. Bernier-Grand with a sense of responsibility and pride. I wanted to portray a very personal, close, vivid César Chávez, as well as the halo of myth that his life generates. I was happy to see this book being honored by the Pura Belpré Honor Award.

My Name Is Celia: The Life of Celia Cruz/
Me llamo Celia: La vida de Celia Cruz
Rafael López

Celia Cruz was the queen of Latin music, breaking down racial and cultural barriers with her exceptional talent, passion, and perseverance. *Celia* was also my first book out of the starting gate. Getting a Pura Belpré Honor fueled deep-rooted aspirations and grew my confidence to pursue the enduring dream of illustrating children's books. My son once told me that he believed my paintbrushes were magic wands. I was determined to use them to tell diverse stories that authentically reflected the richness of my own heritage. It is important to me that diverse children would see themselves in the pages of books I illustrate and this honor encouraged and ignited that intent.

2004 Narrative Medal Winner

Julia Álvarez

Before we were Free

Before we were Free was born out of gratitude. It is dedicated "to those who stayed." In 1960 when my family escaped from the Dominican Republic to the United States, we left behind cousins, *tías*, *tíos*, friends, and their families. In fact, we left behind a whole country bearing the brunt of that last, brutal year of a thirty-one-year dictatorship. This book was born out of gratitude to all those who stayed and fought for freedom.

After the dictatorship in the Dominican Republic ended, I'd return for visits, and my uncle would take me aside. He had gone to Yale as a young man. By then I had become identified as "*la escritora*" in the family. "One day," my uncle would say, "we're going to write a book together. The title is going to be *I Learned More in Jail than at Yale*." He died before we could undertake this joint project. But when I sat down to write *Before we were Free*, I e-mailed his son and asked what he remembered of those days before his father was captured and afterwards, when they lived in fear, not knowing if they would ever see my uncle alive again. Many mornings before starting to write, I'd sit reading his e-mails and sobbing in front of the computer. Some of my uncle's and my cousin's memories found their way into my book.

I wanted to write a story about growing up in a dictatorship so that young readers could experience that world and remember it. I believe that the memory of having been someone else—in other words, the act of reading—can be a force for peace. I wanted to bring young readers into the world of a dictatorship as seen from the eyes of another young person. I wanted young readers to experience firsthand the enormous cost of becoming a free person.

I thank the Association for Library Services to Children and REFORMA for honoring *Before we were Free*. By recognizing works that portray, affirm, and celebrate our rich *cultura* and *historia*, you enrich all of us in the family of readers.

Yuyi Morales

Just a Minute
A Trickster Tale and Counting Book

There is nothing like receiving a Pura Belpré call. I had seen books at the public library that sported the medal. Alma Flor Ada's *Under the Royal Palms* was a book I remembered having the seal—Alma Flor, who had once given me the chance to attend her class in writing children's literature at USF for free, and who, to my disbelief, once looked at me in the eyes in one of her classes and told me, "You are a writer."

I have devoured books with the medal, because I was fascinated with the fact that the Pura Belpré Award celebrated something that I didn't think anybody did in the United States. It celebrated being Latino.

I come from Mexico—a country that, when conquered by the Spaniards, suffered the near annihilation of its indigenous population. And what the conquest didn't subjugate in the body, it subjugated in the heart. Indigenous people were indoctrinated to accept the status of powerless children who were good for very little. They were taught to offer servitude and admiration to others—those who had light skin, who came from another country, or who spoke another language. This conquest of the identity of indigenous Mexicans is something I grew up with, and I believed it. When I migrated to the United States, my conquered heart feared for my limitations: the color of my skin, my inability to speak English, and certainly my limited intellect and creativity. That is how I saw myself.

When I received the call from the Pura Belpré Committee, something profound changed for me. Here was a group of U.S. librarians cheering for the first book I had created, *Just A Minute*, the story of a brown grandmother who opens her door one morning to find a skeleton waiting for her. When I submitted my book for publication, I received many letters from editors telling me how much they liked my illustrations, but that my story was scary; children would not want to open the book, parents would not want to buy it. Perhaps this is true, for not all books are for everyone. However, the day that the Pura Belpré Award Committee called me, they were telling me that my book was valid, that my work had quality, and that my identity—which for so long I had believed to work against me—was something to be celebrated.

2004 Honor Books for Narrative

Cuba 15
Nancy Osa

Earning the Belpré Honor gave me personal and professional validation early in my writing career. The medal meant that my Cuban and American sides combined to form a valuable voice in literature. It let my editors know that they were right to publish and promote my book. It let teachers and parents know that they should encourage children to read it. Perhaps most important, honor status has kept my book in print during a time of daunting changes in the writing and publishing worlds. Thanks to the Belpré Honor, *Cuba 15* will live to enrich new generations of young readers.

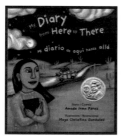

My Diary from Here to There/ Mi diario de aquí hasta allá
Amada Irma Pérez

My Diary from Here to There/Mi diario de aquí hasta allá connects children of immigrants and nonimmigrants alike. The story about my family's immigration from Mexico to the United States includes universal themes of family, love, friendship, struggle, separation, and a girl's adjustment to a new life. Strong memories of change inspired me. The Pura Belpré Committee recognized my book as worthy of this important award and elevated its significance in children's literature. Now it's in students' hands! The seal shines brightly on the book's cover as it sheds light on the plight of millions of immigrants.

2004 Honor Books for Illustration

First Day in Grapes
Robert Casilla

Having *First Day in Grapes* chosen as a 2004 Pura Belpré Honor Book was very special and a bit ironic to me. Early on there were no awards that I knew of that recognized books by authors and illustrators of Latino heritage. I thought that such an award would generate more books about Hispanic children, their families, and their culture. I voiced this concern to my friend Toni Parker who was the director of Black Books Galore at the time. A few months later around 1996 she called me and informed me that an award called the Pura Belpré Award had been established. After hearing the great news, I made it a point to learn about Pura Belpré and what she meant to Latino children's literature.

Harvesting Hope: The Story of César Chavez
Yuyi Morales

I received the manuscript for *Harvesting Hope* one day in the mail. I had been asked if I would be interested in illustrating this story about César Chavez. Of course I would, this would be my first trade book, a dream come true! But…who was César Chavez? Illustrating this book took me on a journey of traveling and learning about César, a timid child of gentle manners who grew up to become the strong and peaceful leader of the farmworkers in the United States. César Chavez, brown like me, became my hero.

The Pot That Juan Built
David Díaz

When I first heard of this project, I thought it was going to be a traditional tale, which I love to illustrate. However, when I realized it was a true story, I became drawn to the charismatic character of Juan Quezada, to the town of Mata Ortíz, and to the art of pottery. As I researched the art of the people of *Casas Grandes*, I became more and more fascinated by the means and method of their art to create beautiful pottery. I was happy to see that the book that Nancy Andrews-Goebel wrote was noticed and recognized by the Pura Belpré Committee.

2002 Narrative Medal Winner

Pam Muñoz Ryan

Esperanza Rising

Esperanza Rising parallels my grandmother's immigration story from Aguascalientes, Mexico, to the segregated farm labor camps in California. It is my family's story—a riches-to-rags story, which is a common thread in some immigrants' stories, no matter their country of birth.

When *Esperanza Rising* won the Pura Belpré Medal in 2002, the award was bestowed every other year, so I received the news eighteen months after publication. It was an unexpected surprise and validation for me, my publisher, and my readers.

All children deserve to have stories with which they can identify or escape, either compelling stories they can "fall into" or a story that reflects their own culture or circumstance. In a perfect world, your ethnicity should not hold you back. It should thrust your forward, giving you a rich well of stories, language, and history from which you can draw and reap. But we do not live in that world. Prejudices, misconceptions, and stereotypes still exist, however veiled. We cannot simply look into another person's eyes and understand him or her. We must look into other people's stories before we can accept differences or celebrate our similar humanity. The Pura Belpré Award has illuminated the writers who plant the seeds of perspective and pride.

Today, *Esperanza Rising* has been in print for sixteen years. Many people have asked whether I had trouble getting the story published because it was about diverse characters. I was fortunate to have an editor, Tracy Mack, and a publisher, Scholastic, who embraced the story from the onset and who were consistently collaborative and enthusiastic. The publication was followed by the Pura Belpré Medal, which brought *Esperanza Rising* to the attention of people who might not have known about or read the book. And when a book is brought to the attention of librarians, educators, and booksellers, it can't help but affect readership. That was how this distinguished award significantly affected my authorship: It has helped sustain the life of the book in print. For that, I am deeply grateful.

Susan Guevara

Chato and the Party Animals

Illustrating Chato's second adventure allowed me to explore the serious accusation that I condoned gang behavior by how I dressed the cool low-riding cats of *Chato's Kitchen*. Their baggy pants, backwards baseball caps, and red bandanas seemed to mimic those children in, or dead because of, a gang.

"What is a gang and how can I understand it?" was the question the book asked of me this time. This is a world I know nothing about. How do I be honest about my experience yet answer the question? I had to speak about what I do know, truly belonging to a family. I know what it is to feel safe, accepted, and loved beyond my mistakes. A family is what Novio Boy was missing. Who doesn't wish to be part of some group, some place that is safe and welcoming?

The work of artists Marc Chagall and Frida Kahlo helped me use visual metaphor and magical realism to show Novio Boy's transition as he discovers that Chato and the longtime neighborhood friends are his family. They are his *Árbol de la vida*—his Tree of Life rooting him to the earth. They know him and love him, and he is one of them.

There is a Nahua concept that we are born with a physical heart and face, but that as artists, poets, musicians, and priests, we must create a deified heart and a true face. We must combine the two to shine a true reflection of who we are. Heart-making and face-making give us strength. No more masking ourselves with others' expectations.

Art-making combines my heart and my face. I can only speak truthfully about what I know. If I am uncertain about my subject, I have to explore it until I do know. Though it often frightens me to start without knowing where I will end, I love this process. I love the questions it asks of me. And it is by this deep trust and affection for the process that I have gifted myself to you, and shown you my true face.

2002 Honor Books for Narrative

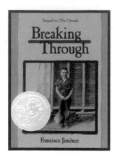

Breaking Through
Francisco Jiménez

I wrote *Breaking Through* to pay tribute to my teachers and to document part of my family's history but, more importantly, to voice the experiences of many children and young adults, especially Latinos, who confront numerous obstacles in their efforts to get an education. How they manage to break through depends as much on their courage, hope, and God-given talents as it does on loving compassionate and generous people who commit themselves to making a difference in the lives of children and young adults. I also wrote it to honor the community of my childhood: farm workers whose lives and hard and noble work are for the most part invisible and whose courage, hopes, and dreams for a better life for their children, and their children's children, give meaning to the term "the American dream." Their story is the American story.

Iguanas in the Snow and Other Winter Poems/ Iguanas en la nieve y otros poemas de invierno
Francisco X. Alarcón (1954–2016)

To receive the then biennial
Pura Belpré Honor Award
for the third consecutive time

for my fourth book of poems
for children *Iguanas in the Snow
and Other Winter Poems*

was like tasting the delicious
cherry on the very top of a cake;
it was both satisfying and humbling,

satisfying that the power of poetry
in its bilingual mode could cross
all boundaries and be recognized,

humbling that a poetry practitioner
like me could be so honored by peers,
fellow travelers on the same path;

with this award under my wing
I felt like a happy iguana sliding
on the winter slope of a snow hill

© *Francisco X. Alarcón*

Juan Bobo Goes to Work
Joe Cepeda

I had never heard of Juan Bobo before I read Marisa Montes's manuscript. I soon found out what a beloved character he was… and how much fun I would have illustrating one of his misadventures. I laughed and painted at the same time. Juan Bobo was built for comedy, and it was a delight to help add to such a wonderful part of traditional Latino literary culture. I've always been proud of my Chicano roots. To be included on the list of Pura Belpré honorees adds to a fulfilling professional life as a Latino working in a craft that I so cherish.

2000 Narrative Medal Winner

Alma Flor Ada

Under the Royal Palms

Portraying the diversity and richness of the Latino experience is an ongoing theme in my work and in the books I have coauthored with Isabel Campoy. Yet while some underlying principles inform everything I write, each book's creation follows its own unique path.

Three interwoven elements gave birth to *Under the Royal Palms*.

One was the interest awakened by *Where the Flame Trees Bloom*, my earlier book of childhood memories. As young people search for a greater understanding of life, they want to learn about those who came before them. Many teachers have encouraged their students to write about their own families and childhood experiences after reading *Where the Flame Trees Bloom*. Their appreciative messages confirmed the value of this style of memoirs.

I also received encouragement from my friend, the great artist Antonio Martorell, who illustrated *Where the Flame Trees Bloom*. Reminding me that I had ended that book by saying that these were only a few of the many stories that nestled among the trees of my childhood memories, he suggested I write the rest.

A third powerful source of motivation came from within: the desire to honor those who had nurtured my growing-up years and to share their stories with a new generation of readers. Re-creating the past so it can live on in the present and perhaps inspire others in the future is one of the reasons why *Under the Royal Palms* was written.

My joy in having this book receive the Pura Belpré Medal was deepened by the mention of *Where the Flame Trees Bloom* in the award committee's commendation. I experienced this as a recognition of the significance of sharing our own personal histories with authenticity.

Now, sixteen years later, *Under the Royal Palms* and *Where the Flame Trees Bloom* will appear together in one volume, along with *Days at La Quinta Simoni*, a new collection of childhood stories. This new book, *Island Treasures*, is enriched by numerous family photographs. It is a tribute by Atheneum, the book's publisher, to the value that Latino experiences can have for all readers.

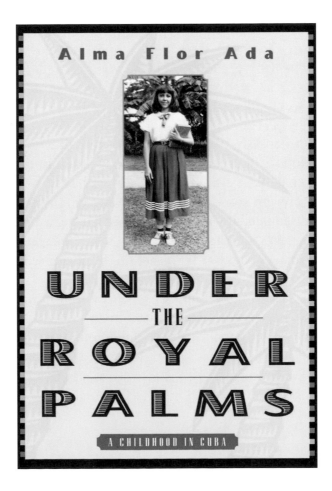

Carmen Lomas Garza

Magic Windows/ Ventanas mágicas

The inspiration for *Magic Windows* came from the *banderitas de papel picado* (tissue paper cutouts) of my youth. Each paper cutout hanging on a string across a room, a street, or a backyard became a window for my imagination.

As a child, I watched my grandmother and mother fold paper and then cut it with scissors to create patterns to be traced onto fabric for embroidering. I realized that I, too, could create designs.

As a young adult in the early 1970s, I progressed into drawing scenes on heavier paper to cut with knives in order to make the paper cutout be the final artwork. I quickly realized that every element in the design had to be connected to each other in order to prevent some sections from flopping over. And because it is very difficult to erase pencil lines once the paper has been cut I drew the images on the back of the paper so that the front side would be clean. That also meant I had to draw the images backwards so that the front side would read correctly.

Computerized laser-cutting technology gave me the opportunity to publish some of my paper cutouts as limited-edition metal cutouts that can hang from the ceiling or on a wall, and to produce metal cutout fences and security walls.

Most of my paper and metal cutouts, paintings, and prints depict my childhood memories of our Mexican-American community in South Texas. I create images that elicit recognition and appreciation among Mexican-Americans, both adults and children, while at the same time serving as a source of education for others not familiar with our culture. It has been my objective since 1969 to instill pride in our history and culture in American society.

2000 Honor Books for Narrative

From the Bellybutton of the Moon and Other Summer Poems/Del ombligo de la Luna y otros poemas de verano
Francisco X. Alarcón (1954–2016)

I felt I was the Moon
upon learning about
this award for my book

*From the Bellybutton
of the Moon and Other
Summer Poems*

The Pura Belpré Honor Award
was more than an honor,
it was a recognition

coming from the bellybutton
of our culture and heritage,
from the guardians

of the temples of knowledge,
the keepers of books, treasures
of our community libraries

how sweet to share this award
with my friend Juan Felipe Herrera,
for his *Laughing Out Loud, I Fly*

yes, I flew from the Earth
to the Moon, and then back
happy to be alive on this Earth

© Francisco X. Alarcón

Laughing Out Loud, I Fly: Poems in English and Spanish
Juan Felipe Herrera

I wrote *Laughing Out Loud, I Fly* in my brother-in-law's sizzling kitchen during Thanksgiving in San José, California. The fragrance of well-served dinner plates and my pocketbook-sized copy of Picasso's poems about his childhood urged me to the point of non-stop, super-fast scribbling for over three hours. Time snapped when I finished several notebooks with nervous, cryptic scrawls of words and numbers. Then I thought maybe no one will make sense out of it—until I received the Pura Belpré Author Honor Award in 2000. I thank you, for believing in me.

2000 Honor Books for Illustration

Barrio: José's Neighborhood
George Ancona

I grew up in Coney Island. We were the only family that spoke Spanish in the neighborhood. I heard Italian, Polish, Yiddish, German, and Russian on the streets and in the homes of friends, but no Spanish. When I got to San Fransisco and wandered around the Barrio and I heard Spanish all around me, I was smitten by the experience. I wanted to know more about growing up in the United States surrounded by Spanish all around me. It was a joy. Then I met José in one of the schools, got to know his family, and knew I had to do the book.

Mama & Papa Have a Store
Amelia Lau Carling

The Pure Belpré Award recognizes the multidimensionality of Latino culture beautifully. In *Mama & Papa Have a Store*, I set out to capture a moment when a child only knows the people, the place, the smells, the colors, and all the sensations around her—and when every day seems commonplace. In the course of one day in my parents' store, that of a Chinese family living in Guatemala, many layers of experience are nonetheless revealed. The day in the store reflects on migration stories, cross-cultural encounters, child's play, and family life in the quiet backwater of a small Latin American city.

The Secret Stars
Felipe Dávalos

We have in our Latino cultural tradition beautiful celebrations in which all the members of our families participate together. Such is the case for Three Kings' Day, where the Kings come at the end of the twelve days of Christmas to bring kids presents. I was invited to illustrate a book called *The Secret Stars* by Joseph Slate about how on a dark and rainy night, the Three Kings find their way to children's homes. To do those paintings was very rewarding, but to be told that the book was selected as a Pura Belpré Illustration Honor Book was like a gift from the Kings. Thanks for that great present!

1998 Narrative Medal Winner

Victor Martínez
(1954–2011)

Parrot in the Oven
Mi vida

Joanna Cotler, formerly of HarperCollins, had this to say about Victor Martínez:

Victor described himself as irascible, but I found him to be a brilliant, lovely man. When his genius of an editor, Heather Henson, first gave me his manuscript to read I fell in love with it and knew we had to publish it. The night before Victor's book was nominated for the National Book Award, he told me he had planned to give up writing. I am so glad he changed his mind. Victor died in 2011 of lung cancer. Here's what his editor, Heather Henson, had to say about him:

As soon as I read the manuscript for *Parrot in the Oven* I was hooked. The voice was powerful. It gripped me. Immediately I felt the honesty and authenticity of the story. There was a rawness, and yet a tenderness too, a lyricism that felt new, fresh. Victor Martinez was a poet—that was clear to me from the moment I began reading his work. He was describing some very real, very gritty experiences of growing up Chicano in America—immigrant parents, pressures of gang life, struggles with poverty and finding your place—but he was doing it with a beauty and grace that could simply, in certain moments, take your breath away.

The week before the National Book Awards, we brought Victor from San Francisco to New York City. I would go on talks with him to the roughest parts of the city, the toughest schools in the Bronx and Brooklyn. I was amazed by the response from teens. All these tough kids who (their teachers told us) had never wanted to read before, they were picking up Victor's book and actually talking about it in class. They were engaging in our discussions. I realized it's because they saw themselves there, in the pages of that book. They were able to identify with the characters. The book was true and real to them, to their world. The awards Victor received for *Parrot in the Oven* were amazing. But the real prize for me, and I think for him too, was seeing what a huge impact his story had on kids, on a whole population who had never seen their own stories in print before.

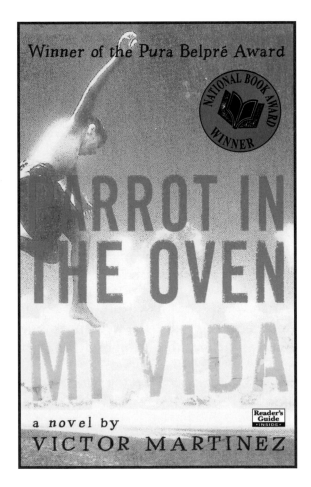

Stephanie García

Snapshots from the Wedding

I was a rambunctious child. One day after skipping home from school, I ran through the back door of our house on Easton Street and flung my books down on the floor of the laundry room. Overcome by the sweet and slightly pungent smell coming from our oven, I crept quietly to it, opening the door ever so slightly. Then I opened the door wide. I was shocked by what I saw. Two black beady eyes were staring at me—out of the head of a carcass! I took a breath and passed out on the spot. The next thing I remember was Mom saying, "Little stinker, it's just *cabeza*." Later that evening, we all enjoyed eating soft tacos with cilantro, salsa, a dab of Mom's awesome guacamole, and "*la cabeza*!" This story is one of many memories I use as a reference for my art.

I cherish my culture and the many experiences that have made me who I am—unique, Hispanic, Latina, Chicana, and American. These facets are the keystone of my work and embrace the Latino experience. The inspiration for *Snapshots from the Wedding* was my beloved Aunt Esther's wedding. Aunt Esther also was my nanny. She married when I was five. Knowing how important she was to me, she asked me to be her flower girl. The wedding was very much like Gary's manuscript. My aunt was the most beautiful bride I had ever seen—both then and since.

The magic of that day, as I walked down the aisle dropping petals of roses, has always been in my heart. Now it lives in the form of my artwork. Sliding down the hallway in our socks, drinking soda and eating chips, waiting for the fantastic cake to be cut so that we could eat roses made of frosting—all of those beautiful memories are now shared with many.

I am grateful to everyone who has worked hard to bring my work, as well as the work of all of the other Latino authors and illustrators, to the attention of the public through the Pura Belpré Award.

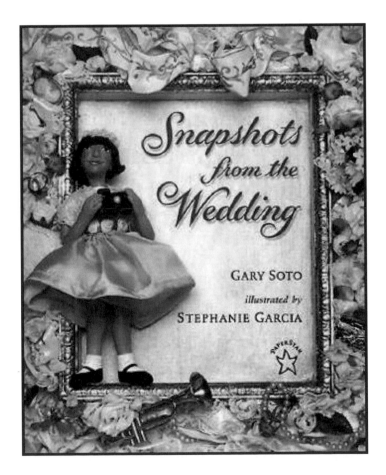

1998 Honor Books for Narrative

Laughing Tomatoes and Other Spring Poems/
Jitomates Risueños y otros poemas de primavera
Francisco X. Alarcón (1954–2016)

This award for *Laughing Tomatoes and Other Spring Poems*, my first book of bilingual poems for children made me laugh out so loud

I felt so proud, cheerful, and round
as the laughing tomatoes in my book.
I was so happy to share the spotlight
with the winner of the narrative award,

my close friend, Víctor Martínez, author
of *Parrot in the Oven: Mi Vida*,
with whom I shared so many things in
life, like exact same birthdays and then,
these awards.

This award made possible four other
books of poems celebrating the stations
of the year.
For that, I am forever thankful.
Muchas gracias.

© *Francisco X. Alarcón*

Spirits of the High Mesa

Floyd Martínez (1941–2013)

A native of New Mexico, Floyd Martínez had a lifelong interest in fiction and wrote various short stories. *Spirits of the High Mesa* is his first published novel. As a Latino writer, his "storytelling" perspective is interesting and refreshing. His interest in writing originated from his family and heritage, and it was obvious in his reminiscences about his inspirations as a writer:

"I am the self-appointed legacy of those who came before me who were readers, storytellers, and surely good liars. Fiction is the art of blending how things are with how we would want them to be. Writing fiction requires the unleashing of the imagination to work its contained magic and yet sculpturing the product into an engrossing and believable story…And the ultimate pleasure is to produce a story that others will enjoy."

1998 Honor Books for Illustration

Gathering the Sun: An Alphabet in Spanish and English
Simón Silva

In 1998 I was the recipient of the Pura Belpré Honor Book Award for illustrating the book *Gathering the Sun*. This recognition meant for me the acknowledgement not just of the merits of my art, but of the dignity, pride, and honor of my people— Latino farmworkers in the United States. The book, written by Alma Flor Ada, continues to be in print eighteen years later, and every day I find a new child who tells me, "That is me on page…" Nothing could be more rewarding than to be embraced by a common identity with the readers!

The Golden Flower: A Taíno Myth from Puerto Rico
Enrique O. Sánchez

I was honored with the Pura Belpré Honor Award for illustrating *The Golden Flower: A Taíno Myth from Puerto Rico*. It is a story of how water came to the world and how the island of Puerto Rico was created.

On receiving the award in 1998, I talked about how much I enjoyed working on the book, and that Pura Belpré would have appreciated this book, since she wrote and collected many folktales from Puerto Rico and published them as children's books. Pura was also a puppeteer, and my characters in the book look puppet-like with angular bodies and painted faces.

In My Family/ En mi familia
Carmen Lomas Garza

Dancing, hitting a piñata, eating sweet turnovers, and feeding horned toads—these are more of my childhood memories in South Texas that are in my paintings in my second children's picture book, *In My Family/En mi familia*. My paintings are a celebration of our Mexican-American culture and history. I have been an artist since the age of thirteen, and I hope that when Latinos see familiarity in my artwork they will feel pride in their own stories. Readers not familiar with the subject can get a better understanding of our every day lives and join in the celebration.

1996 Narrative Medal Winner

Judith Ortíz Cofer

An Island Like You
Stories of the Barrio

When I first felt my hunger for books, I did not know that I was reading to find out who I was. I only knew that stories transported me into unknown worlds through the minds and hearts of characters who were as different as they were distant from me, an adolescent Puerto Rican girl growing up in New Jersey, a place so different from my native island that it might as well have been another planet. No wonder that as a teenager I immersed myself in science fiction—Ray Bradbury's *The Martian Chronicles* and, later, Ursula K. LeGuin's *The Left Hand of Darkness*. Bradbury and LeGuin helped me navigate my alienation and imagine my way into alternate identities. With a mere flick of the page and my imagination, I could become anyone, anywhere; yet, I still longed to find a version of me, a reflection of us, in a book. So I began to write about my own bicultural reality—as Toni Morrison said, "If there's a book that you want to read, but it hasn't been written yet, then you must write it"—and I found that literature becomes universal, transcending culture and language, when it reflects one's real, complex human experience. Books are not only mirrors, but also windows.

I decided I could and should write for young adults when I visited the schools where my work was being read. I realized that today's bicultural teenagers are caught not only between cultures and languages, but also between the worlds of childhood and adulthood. When writing *An Island Like You: Stories of the Barrio*, it was my goal to give each teenage character a moment of revelation about who she or he is. I am pleased and amazed that the book is still being read in classrooms and by thousands of young people across the country. Having been awarded the very first Pura Belpré Award continues to encourage me to write for children and younger readers—sharing our stories, our experience of growing up Latina/o in the United States.

1996 Illustration Medal Winner

Susan Guevara

Chato's Kitchen

I began my bookmaking career when there was a dearth of titles set in Latino culture. How lucky to receive a manuscript that had the *chispa*, the internal spark needed to warrant a year of my life. *Chato's Kitchen* by Gary Soto was fiery! It was spicy! It was a conflagration of originality and color. Its language blasted the boundaries of what picture book writing had been.

Art making is an exploration. A question is asked. *Chato's Kitchen* asked me about my heritage and my history. The manuscript included Chicano slang and voiced the world and history of its author, Gary Soto. How would I illustrate this world if I hadn't lived it as Gary had? Who am I in this world and how do I put that into my paintings? I looked outside of myself for the answers; to books, to movies, to pop culture, to Mexican and Mexican-American history and artists, to the city of Los Angeles, to my father's Mexican heritage, the list goes on and on. Finally, I was forced to look at what I value most in my own life. That list is succinct and my gratitude for my life is eternal.

I value my family and friends. I value putting my love into the food I cook for them. I value the sky, the earth, and all the living things and beings on it. I value literacy and the tools reading, writing, and critical thinking give us to create peace. I value my curiosity and my love of learning all things new and foreign. I value my body, my eyes, my hands, and most of all, my heart and mind from which I am able to envision the specific world of a book manuscript and share it with you in my illustrations.

The recognition of the first Pura Belpré Committee for this book moved me to understand the responsibilities I have as an artist. I must be honest and unflinching in what I know inside myself to be true. This has been one of the best lessons of my art-making life.

1996 Honor Books for Narrative

Baseball in April and Other Stories
Gary Soto

The Mexican-American author Gary Soto draws on his own experience growing up in California's Central Valley to craft a collection of eleven wonderful short stories. The kids in these stories are Latino, but we can all identify with their dreams and aspirations.

The Bossy Gallito/El gallo de bodas
A Traditional Cuban Folktale
Lucía González

I left Cuba as a child with no material possessions except an imagination richly populated with characters from the stories told to me by my *tía abuela*, la Nena. Those stories became part of my cultural essence and my inspiration to write. Stories are immigrants just as are the people who bring them. I needed to document my stories, to write them for the children of my children. That is why I wrote *The Bossy Gallito/El gallo de bodas*.

The Bossy Gallito/El gallo de bodas
A Traditional Cuban Folktale
Lulu Delacre

The first time I read Lucía's retelling of *El Gallo de Bodas*, I fell in love with it. It had such a Cuban flavor that I immediately heard the *gallito* speaking in the voice of my Cuban father-in-law. The story begged to be set in a Cuban community. Unable to go to Cuba for the ideal setting, I went to Miami. Lucía supplied photos of *gallos de pelea* and tips on which church to depict and which to go to in order to witness a traditional Cuban wedding.

Family Pictures/ Cuadros de familia
Carmen Lomas Garza

My paintings are recollections of my childhood memories in South Texas that celebrate our Mexican-American culture and history in the United States. My words in *Family Pictures/Cuadros de familia* introduce the paintings, and the viewer sees the rest of the short story in the details. It has been my hope since the age of thirteen that when Latinos see familiarity in my artwork they will feel pride in their own stories. Readers not familiar with the subject can get a better understanding of our every day lives and join in the celebration.

Pablo Remembers: The Fiesta of the Day of the Dead
George Ancona

I went to Mexico for the first time when I graduated high school. There, I got to meet my grandparents, aunts, uncles, and cousins. When I saw the festival of the Day of the Dead, I was impressed that even dead relatives are visited, celebrated, and remembered. When people spend a lifetime living close together—be it next door, across the street, or a few blocks away—they will be missed. The Day of the Dead affirms the love and respect for loved ones who are gone but still in our lives.

About the Award Winners

ADA, ALMA FLOR

Alma Flor Ada, professor emerita at the University of San Francisco, has devoted her life to advocacy for peace by promoting a pedagogy oriented to personal realization and social justice. A former Radcliffe scholar at Harvard University and a Fulbright research scholar, she is an internationally renowned speaker. Dr. Ada's numerous children's books of poetry, narrative, folklore, and nonfiction have received many prestigious awards, such as the Christopher Medal, Pura Belpré Medal, Parent's Choice Honor, and NCSS and CBC Notable Books, among many others. In 2012, she received the Virginia Hamilton Literary Award in recognition of her body of work for children.

AGOSÍN, MARJORIE

Marjorie Agosín is the Luella LaMer Slaner Professor of Latin American studies at Wellesley College. She is an award-winning poet and also a human rights activist. She has been recognized both in North and South America as a prolific and versatile author who has written poetry, memoirs, nonfiction, and her first YA novel. Agosín has received many awards for her creative work as well as her human rights work. In 2015, she received the Pura Belpré Award for *I Lived on Butterfly Hill*. She shares her time between Wellesley Massachusetts; Ogunquit, Maine; and Costa Brava, Chile.

ALARCÓN, FRANCISCO X.

Francisco X. Alarcón (1954–2016), award-winning Chicano poet and educator, was born in Los Angeles, grew up in Guadalajara, Mexico, and lived in Davis, California, where he taught at the University of California. He was a three-time recipient of the Pura Belpré Honor Award. He was the author of three other poetry books for children and six volumes of poetry for adults, for which he received numerous awards and recognition.

ÁLVAREZ, JULIA

Shortly after she was born, in 1950, Julia Álvarez's parents moved back to the Dominican Republic from New York City. A versatile writer, Julia Álvarez has written novels, collections of poems, and numerous books for young readers. Álvarez has won numerous awards for her work, including the Pura Belpré, the Américas Award, the Hispanic Heritage Award in Literature, and the F. Scott Fitzgerald Award for Outstanding Achievement in American Literature. She is currently a writer in residence at Middlebury College in Vermont. Álvarez and her husband, Bill Eichner, in 1997 established Alta Gracia, a sustainable coffee farm and literacy center in the mountains of the Dominican Republic.

ANCONA, GEORGE

George Ancona grew up in Coney Island, Brooklyn, New York. Both his parents came from Yucatán, Mexico, and met in New York City. Ancona grew up in an immigrant neighborhood where they were the only Spanish-speaking family. His father's hobby was photography, and it was Ancona's first introduction to the making of images. Ancona began making children's books with his photographs and the words of other writers. Eventually, he began writing his own books. Now through his incredible photographs and words, he can share his experiences with young readers.

BERNIER-GRAND, CARMEN T.

Carmen T. Bernier-Grand is the author of eleven books for children and young adults. Her books *César: ¡Sí, se puede! Yes, We Can!* and *Diego: Bigger Than Life* have been Oregon Book Award finalists. Those two biographies and her book *Frida: ¡Viva la vida! Long Live Life!* received the Pura Belpré Honor for Narrative in 2006, 2010, and 2008 respectively. Her biography *Alicia Alonso: Prima Ballerina* received starred reviews from *Booklist* and *Publishers Weekly* and was a 2012 Notable Book for Global Society. Bernier-Grand teaches at Writers in the Schools, a program of Oregon Literary Arts, and at the MFA Workshop program of Northwest Institute of Literary Arts at Whidbey Island, in Washington State.

BOWLES, DAVID

David Bowles comes from a mixed family—Mexican American on his father's side, Anglo on his mother's. He grew up mainly in the Rio Grande Valley, listening to *cuentos* at the knee of his grandmother Garza or on the ranch with his *tíos* and dad. His wife is from Mexico, so the lore he learned from her family in Monterrey added another layer of fascination with his *raíces*, which he began to follow deeper and deeper, researching Aztec and Mayan culture, language, and religion. Now, when he teaches or writes, this *mestizaje* of traditions infuses and transforms his modern techniques and sensibilities.

CANALES, VIOLA

Viola Canales grew up in a Spanish-speaking household in McAllen, Texas. At the age of fifteen, she attended St. Stephen's Episcopal School in Austin, followed by Harvard College and later Harvard Law School. She has been a captain in the U.S. Army, a litigator, and an official in the Clinton administration. She has published a short story collection, *Orange Candy Slices and Other Secret Tales* (2001), and a YA novel, *The Tequila Worm* (2005), for which she won the Pura Belpré Medal for Narrative in 2006.

CARLING, AMELIA LAU

Amelia Lau Carling was born and raised in Guatemala City. Her parents were Chinese immigrants who owned a general store there from the 1940s to the early 1980s, while raising a family of six. Carling attended Occidental College in California, majoring in art. She has worked as a book designer, art director, and design manager for various publishing houses in New York City and has authored and illustrated several children's books. She currently lives in Westchester County, New York.

CASILLA, ROBERT

Robert Casilla was born in Jersey City, New Jersey, to Puerto Rican parents. Although he grew up in New Jersey, he attended fourth grade in Puerto Rico. His formal art training took place at the School of Visual Arts in New York City, where he earned a BFA degree. Since 1984, Casilla has worked as a freelance illustrator. He has illustrated more than thirty children's books, many of which are picture book biographies. He has also illustrated many multicultural children's books. Casilla works from his home in New Fairfield, Connecticut, where he lives with his wife and two children.

CASTRO, ANTONIO L.

Antonio Castro López (L.) was born in Zacatecas, Mexico, and has lived in the Juárez-El Paso area for most of his life. He has illustrated dozens of children's books, including *Barry, the Bravest Saint Bernard* (Random House), *Pájaro Verde, Treasure on Gold Street, The Day It Snowed Tortillas,* and *Gum-Chewing Rattler* (Cinco Puntos Press). In 2005, the government of the state of Chihuahua, Mexico, commissioned Castro to paint a mural for the government palace. The mural commemorates the anniversary of the Battle of Tomochic. His work has been exhibited in galleries and museums in Texas, Mexico City, Spain, and Italy.

CEPEDA, JOE

Joe Cepeda received his BFA in illustration from California State University, Long Beach, in 1992 and also studied engineering at Cornell University. He is the illustrator of award-winning picture books such as *What a Truly Cool World* (Scholastic), *Nappy Hair* (Knopf), and *Mice and Beans* (Scholastic), as well as *The Swing* (Arthur A. Levine Books), which he wrote as well as illustrated. Mr. Cepeda was selected to illustrate the cover of Shaquille O'Neal and Reading Is Fundamental's Biggest Children's Book in the World. He received a Pura Belpré Honor Award in 2002. His work has been accepted to the Society of Illustrators' shows in New York and Los Angeles. In addition to his illustrative work, Mr. Cepeda is sought after as a public speaker for schools and other groups. He is the current president of the Society of Illustrators of Los Angeles. He lives in Southern California with his wife and son.

COLÓN, RAÚL

Raúl Colón was born in New York City in December 1952 and moved with his parents in the 1960s to Caguas, Puerto Rico, where he studied commercial art. In 1988, Colón settled with his family in New City, New York, and began a freelance career. His work has been seen in a range of venues, including the *New York Times*, the *New Yorker*, NYC subways, CDs, and theater posters. He is also an award-winning illustrator of more than thirty books for children. The industry recognized Raúl with a Golden Kite Award and the Pura Belpré Medal in 2006 for his illustration of *Doña Flor: A Tall Tale of a Giant Woman with a Great Big Heart*.

CÓRDOVA, AMY

Amy Córdova is a visual artist, educator, author, and nationally recognized children's book illustrator. She has illustrated eighteen books for children and has written and illustrated two of her own titles. She received the Pura Belpré Honor for Illustration for *What Can You Do with a Rebozo?* in 2009 and for *Fiesta Babies* in 2011. A sense of place, traditional cultural values, and the presence of spirit in everyday life are the core foundations of Córdova's colorful and inspirational artistic vision. She lives in Santa Fe, New Mexico.

DÁVALOS, FELIPE

Felipe Dávalos was born in Mexico City. He graduated from the First School of Visual Communication in Mexico D.F. Following that, he attended the National Institute of Fine Arts, graduating in painting and sculpture. Finally, he attended the National School of Design and Craftsmanship, acquiring a master of applied arts degree.

He has worked as a designer and illustrator for newspapers, magazines, and books. He has also worked with renowned U.S. universities and participated in archaeological research projects, publishing scientific articles in this field. His research work was presented in 2011 in the exhibit Olmec: Colossal Masterworks of Ancient Mexico at the de Young Museum in San Francisco.

DEEDY, CARMEN AGRA

An award-winning author and storyteller, Carmen Agra Deedy is also an accomplished lecturer, having been a guest speaker for the TED Conference, the Library of Congress, and Columbia University. She is also the host of the four-time Emmy-winning children's program *Love That Book!* Deedy spends much of the year traveling across North America and the Caribbean performing for children. They remain, unapologetically, her favorite audiences

DELACRE, LULU

Three-time Pura Belpré Award honoree Lulu Delacre has been writing and illustrating children's books since 1980. Born and raised in Puerto Rico to Argentinean parents, Delacre says her Latino heritage and her life experiences influence her work. Delacre has lectured internationally, served as a juror for the National Book Awards, and exhibited at the Eric Carle Museum of Picture Book Art, among other venues. You can read more at www.luludelacre.com.

DÍAZ, DAVID

Since he was a young boy, David Díaz has seen life from his colored pencils' points. His illustrations tell the stories he has imagined, the pain he has suffered (his mother died when he was sixteen), and the excellence of his craft. He has lived in Florida and Southern California and presently lives in New Orleans, where he devotes his time to art, friendship, and the pursuit of happiness.

DOMINGUEZ, ANGELA

Angela Dominguez was born in Mexico City, grew up in the great state of Texas, and lived in San Francisco. She is the illustrator of *Mango, Abuela, and Me*, the recipient of the 2016 Pura Belpré Honor Book for Illustration. She is the author and illustrator of picture books such as *Let's Go Hugo!*, *Santiago Stays, Knit Together*, and *Maria Had a Little Llama / María tenía una Llamita*, which received the Pura Belpré Illustration Honor. When Dominguez is not in her Brooklyn studio, she teaches at the Academy of Art University, which honored her with their Distinguished Alumni Award in 2013.

ENGEL, MARGARITA

Margarita Engle is the Cuban American author of many young adult verse novels about the island of Cuba, including *The Surrender Tree*, for which received the Pura Belpré Medal and the first Newbery Honor ever awarded to a Latino author. Her other books have also received multiple Pura Belpré Medals and Honors, three Américas Awards, and the Jane Addams Peace Award. She is the 2016 Pura Belpré Medal recipient for *Enchanted Air: Two Cultures, Two Wings: A Memoir*. Another important recognition for *Enchanted Air* was the YALSA Award for Excellence in Non-Fiction for Young Adult Finalist. Engle lives in central California, where she enjoys hiding in the wilderness to help train her husband's search and rescue dogs. Her website is www.margaritaengle.com.

FLORES-GALBIS, ENRIQUE

Born in Havana, Cuba, artist, novelist, and teacher Enrique Flores-Galbis studied art history at New York University Graduate School and painting at the Art Students League and the New York Academy of Art. Flores-Galbis taught at Parsons for fifteen years and at the Visual Arts Center of New Jersey for twenty-eight years. Some of the awards he has received are the New York City Hispanic Arts Achievement Award, the Distinguished Educator Award from the Parsons School of Design, and the Cintas Fellowship for Painting (two-time recipient).

GARCÍA, STEPHANIE

Stephanie García is a native of Southern California and the great-grandniece of Mexican revolutionary Emiliano Zapata. She graduated from Art Center College of Design in Pasadena, California, with a bachelor of fine arts degree and the highest honor of distinction. Her book honors include *Booklist's* Editor's Choice, the Society of Illustrators Best in Children's Book Illustration, and the 1998 Pura Belpré Medal for Illustration of the book *Snapshots from the Wedding*. García now lives both in Los Angeles and the Bay Area.

GARCÍA McCALL, GUADALUPE

Guadalupe García McCall is the author of *Under the Mesquite* (Lee & Low Books), a novel in verse. Her second novel, *Summer of the Mariposas*, was on the 2012 *School Library Journal*'s Best Books of the Year, among other accolades. García was born in Piedras Negras, Coahuila, Mexico. She immigrated with her family to the United States when she was six years old and grew up in Eagle Pass, Texas (the setting of both her novels and most of her poems).

GARZA, XAVIER

Xavier Garza was born in the Rio Grande Valley of Texas. He is an enthusiastic author, artist, teacher, and storyteller whose work is a lively documentation of life, dreams, superstitions, and heroes in the bigger-than-life world of south Texas. He is the author of numerous books, including *Creepy Creatures and Other Cucuys*, *Juan and the Chupacabras*, *Lucha Libre*, and *Maximilian and the Mystery of the Guardian Angel*. He has received prestigious awards such as the Tejas Star Book Award and the Pura Belpré Honor Book Award, among many other awards.

GONZÁLEZ, LUCÍA

Lucía M. González was born in Caimito del Guayabal, Cuba. She came with her parents and sister to the United States at the age of twelve. González started her career in library services in 1991 after receiving a master's degree in library science from the University of South Florida. Regarded as a dynamic bilingual performer and celebrated for her storytelling technique, González is also a prominent figure in the library community and a past president of REFORMA, the National Association to Promote Library and Information Services to Latinos and the Spanish Speaking.

GONZÁLEZ, MAYA CHRISTINA

Maya Christina González is an artist, author, and educator who has written four books and illustrated more than twenty award-winning, multicultural children's books. She has a small independent press and online school where she teaches the art of creating children's books. She lives in San Francisco. Learn more at www.mayagonzalez.com.

GUEVARA, SUSAN

Susan Guevara is a visual storyteller. Her illustrations, paintings, drawings, and sculptures come from her devotion to the details in the world of that particular work. "My father tells me often our lives are like books. We never know if our life book will have one page, many chapters, or even several volumes. At ninety-one, he says we can be grateful for whatever length we are given. There are many narratives in my life book, short stories and long. The beings in these stories, whether of this world or some other, pass each other, interact, and weave a meaning. It is a meaning of my own making, and it is unlimited in scope and complexity."

GUTIÉRREZ, RUDY

Rudy Gutiérrez's art has been described as "Wall Medicine," ancient yet contemporary, urban in a sense and musical in feel. He believes that the highest honor and fulfillment is to inspire and uplift. His art for book covers, magazines, records, CDs, and children's books, as well as his paintings, have appeared worldwide. Gutiérrez's work is perhaps best known for the cover of the multiplatinum smash-hit recording by Santana, *Shaman*, and for a United Postal Service stamp of Jimi Hendrix for the Musical Icon series. Gutiérrez teaches at Pratt Institute and at the Fashion Institute of Technology's Graduate Illustration Program.

HERRERA, JUAN FELIPE

Juan Felipe Herrera is the author of poetry, fiction, nonfiction, children's books, and young adult novels. He has garnered many awards, among them the Guggenheim Fellowship in Poetry, the National Book Critic's Circle Award, and the Latino Fame Award in Poetry. In 2012, Herrera was named California's Poet Laureate and was named U.S. Poet Laureate in 2015.

JIMÉNEZ, FRANCISO

Author and educator Francisco Jiménez emigrated with his family from Tlaquepaque, Mexico, to California, and as a child worked alongside his parents in the fields of California. He received his BA from Santa Clara University and an MA and Ph.D. in Latin American literature from Columbia University under a Woodrow Wilson Fellowship. Dr. Jiménez's books *The Circuit: Stories from the Life of a Migrant Child*, *Breaking Through*, *Reaching Out*, *La Mariposa*, and *The Christmas Gift/ El regalo de Navidad* have won several national literary awards, including the Américas Book Award, the Pura Belpré Honor Book Award, the Tomás Rivera Book Award, the Boston Globe-Horn Book Award, the Reading the World Award, and the Carter C. Woodson National Book Award.

LÁZARO, GEORGINA

Georgina Lázaro was born in San Juan, Puerto Rico. She published her first book, *El flamboyán amarillo*, in 1996. Since then she has written and published more than fifty books in Puerto Rico, the United States, México, and Spain. Lázaro has received numerous international awards, including important awards in Puerto Rico. Lázaro also received the first Pura Belpré Award ever given to a book written in Spanish for *Federico García Lorca*. Lázaro lives with her husband in Ponce, Puerto Rico.

LOMAS GARZA, CARMEN

Carmen Lomas Garza is one of the most prominent Mexican American artists working today. Born and raised in Texas, she now lives in San Francisco, California. Her paintings have traveled all over the United States and Mexico in numerous exhibitions. In 2007, the Los Angeles Unified School District named a prekindergarten through second grade school, the Carmen Lomas Garza Primary Center, in her honor.

LÓPEZ, RAFAEL

In 1997, Rafael López envisioned and led the Urban Art Trail Project that transformed San Diego's blighted East Village with colorful murals, sculptures, and art installations and serves as a model of urban renewal that has been implemented in cities around the nation. He has worked with hundreds of children, families, and community members to create murals and often reclaim blighted neighborhoods around the country. He received the 2016 Pura Belpré Medal for his illustrations of *Drum Dream Girl: How One Girl's Courage Changed Music*, written by Margarita Engle.

MANZANO, SONIA

Sonia Manzano has affected the lives of millions since the early 1970s as the actress who defined the role of María on the acclaimed television series *Sesame Street*. *The Revolution of Evelyn Serrano*, published by Scholastic, was Manzano's first novel and received a Pura Belpré Honor Award for Narrative in 2013. She is also the author of *No Dogs Allowed* and *A Box Full of Kittens*. Manzano's Christmas picture book, *Miracle on 133rd Street*, and memoir, *Becoming Maria: Love and Chaos in the South Bronx*, both came out in 2015.

MARTÍNEZ, FLOYD

A native of New Mexico, Floyd Martínez (1941–2013) spent most of his career as a psychologist working in mental health and drug abuse. He also had a lifelong interest in fiction and wrote various short stories. The novel *Spirits of the High Mesa* (Piñata Books) was his first published novel and received the 1998 Pura Belpré Honor Book Award. As a Latino writer, his "storytelling" perspective is interesting and refreshing.

MARTÍNEZ, VICTOR

Victor L. Martínez (1954–2011) was a Mexican American poet and author. Martínez was born and raised in Fresno, California, the fourth in a family of twelve children. He attended California State University at Fresno and Stanford University. Martínez was awarded the 1996 National Book Award for Young People's Literature for his first novel, *Parrot in the Oven: Mi vida*, and the 1998 Pura Belpré Medal for Narrative for the same book.

MEDINA, MEG

Meg Medina writes picture, middle grade, and young adult fiction books that examine how cultures intersect, as seen through the eyes of young people. Her young adult novel *Yaqui Delgado Wants to Kick Your Ass*, earned the 2014 Pura Belpré Medal for Narrative, among numerous other distinctions. Her other books are *Burn Baby Burn* (Candlewick Press, 2016); *Mango, Abuela, and Me*, a Junior Library Guild selection and a 2016 Pura Belpré Honor for Narrative; *Tía Isa Wants a Car*, winner of the 2012 Ezra Jack Keats New Writers Medal; *The Girl Who Could Silence the Wind*; and *Milagros: Girl from Away*. In 2014, Medina was named one of the CNN 10: Visionary Women in America for her work to support girls, Latino youth, and diversity in children's literature.

MONTES, MARISA

Marisa Montes (1951–2011) was born in Puerto Rico. At the age of four, she began the traveling life of an "army brat" as her family moved to Missouri and then to France, before settling on the Monterey Peninsula of California. She majored in political science at the University of California, Santa Cruz, and earned a law degree from the University of California Hasting College of the Law. After practicing family law for three years, Montes spent ten years writing and editing law books. During that time she began to write books for children, which she continued to do full time until her death in 2011. Montes was married to her husband, David, for thirty-five years.

MORA, PAT

Poet and author Pat Mora has published more than forty award-winning books for adults, teens, and children. Her more than thirty children's books include books in bilingual formats and Spanish editions. An educator and literacy advocate, she founded *Día, El día de los niños, El día de los libros* (*Children's Day, Book Day*), a year-long community and family initiative that honors children and connects them with the joy of books. Annually across the country, April book fiestas reach out creatively to children from all cultures and languages. REFORMA and the Association for Library Services to Children (ALSC) have been major partners. Mora holds two honorary doctorates, is an honorary member of ALA, and is the 2016 Arbuthnot Lecturer.

MORALES, YUYI

Since migrating to the United States from Mexico in 1994, Yuyi Morales has created some of the most celebrated children's books. She is a five-time winner of the Pura Belpré Medal. Other honors include the Américas Award, the Golden Kite Medal, the Christopher Award, the Jane Adams Award, and the Tomás Rivera Book Award. Her book *Viva Frida* received both a 2015 Caldecott Honor and a 2015 Pura Belpré Medal.

ORTÍZ COFER, JUDITH

Judith Ortíz Cofer is the author of several children's and young adult books, among them *Animal Jamboree: Latino Folktales* (2012), *The Poet Upstairs* (2012), *¡A Bailar!* (2011), *Call Me María* (2006), a young adult novel, and a collection of essays, *An Island Like You: Stories of the Barrio*, for which she received the 1996 Pura Belpré Medal for Narrative. In 2010, she was inducted into the Georgia Writers Hall of Fame. Judith Ortíz Cofer is the Regents' and Franklin Professor of English and Creative Writing Emerita at the University of Georgia.

OSA, NANCY

Nancy Osa brings multicultural audiences together to understand one another through humor and imagination. Her book *Cuba 15* (Random House) was recognized in 2004 as a Pura Belpré Author Honor Book, *Booklist* Top Ten First Novel for Youth, YALSA Best Book for Young Adults, Américas Award Honor Book, ALSC Notable Book, and Oregon Book Award Finalist, and received the Delacorte Press Prize for a First Young Adult Novel.

PALACIOS, SARA

Sara Palacios is the recipient of the 2012 Pura Belpré Illustrator Honor for *Marisol McDonald Doesn't Match / Marisol McDonald no combina*, which has been described as "vibrant" and "eclectic." A native of Mexico, Palacios graduated in graphic design in Mexico and then went on to earn BFA and MFA degrees in illustration from the Academy of Art University in San Francisco. She works with a variety of media, such as collage, ink, and digital artwork.

PARRA, JOHN

John Parra is an award-winning illustrator, fine artist, designer, and educator, best known for his award-winning children's books, including *Green Is a Chile Pepper*, *Waiting for the Biblioburro*, and *Gracias / Thanks*. He has received many awards and honors including two Pura Belpré Honors for Illustration, the Américas Award Commended Title, the SCBWI Golden Kite Award, and the Christopher Award, among many others. His book *Marvelous Cornelius: Hurricane Katrina and the Spirit of New Orleans* (written by Phil Bildner, Chronicle Books) published in summer 2015, coincided with the ten-year anniversary of Hurricane Katrina.

PEÑA, MATT DE LA

Matt de la Peña received his MFA in creative writing from San Diego State University and his BA from the University of the Pacific, where he attended school on a full athletic scholarship for basketball. De la Peña is the *New York Times* best-selling author of six critically acclaimed young adult novels, including *Mexican WhiteBoy*, *The Living*, and *The Hunted*, and two award-winning picture books, *A Nation's Hope* and *Last Stop on Market Street*. De la Peña became the first Latino to win the Newbery Medal, considered to be the top award given to the author of the most distinguished contribution to American literature for children, for his picture book *Last Stop on Market Street*, illustrated by Christian Robinson. De la Peña currently lives in Brooklyn, New York, with his family. He teaches creative writing and visits high schools and colleges throughout the country.

PÉREZ, AMADA IRMA

Amada Irma Pérez is an award-winning author and teacher. Her stories are beloved for their humorous details and universal themes of family support, love, and friendship. She speaks at conferences, festivals, libraries, and schools of all levels. In 2003, she cofounded the writing group Women Who Write (WoWW), and she is a consultant with the South Coast Writing Program. She is a member of the Sandra Cisneros Macondo Writers' Workshop, Society of Children's Book Writers and Illustrators (SCBWI), the Ventura County Writers Club, and the Association of Writers and Writing Programs.

RYAN, PAM MUÑOZ

Pam Muñoz Ryan has written more than forty books for young people, including the novels *Esperanza Rising*, *Becoming Naomi León*, *Riding Freedom*, *Paint the Wind*, *The Dreamer*, and most recently, *Echo*, a 2016 Newbery Honor and Odyssey Honor and a *New York Times* best-seller. She is the author recipient of the NEA's Civil and Human Rights Award and the Virginia Hamilton Literary Award for Multicultural Literature and is twice the recipient of the Pura Belpré Medal. Other selected honors include the PEN USA Award, the Américas Award, the Boston Globe-Horn Book Honor, and the Orbis Pictus Award. She holds bachelor's and master's degrees from San Diego State University. She was born and raised in Bakersfield, California, and lives near San Diego with her family. For more information, visit www.PamMunozRyan.com

SÁENZ, BENJAMÍN ALIRE

Benjamín Alire Sáenz is an award-winning poet, novelist, essayist, and children's book author. Sáenz grew up on a cotton farm in New Mexico speaking only Spanish until he started elementary school. Although his education eventually took him to Denver, Belgium, Iowa, and California, Sáenz settled in the border region between Texas and New Mexico. He has won numerous awards for his work.

SÁNCHEZ, ENRIQUE O.

Enrique O. Sánchez is a fine artist and illustrator of children's books. He was born in 1942 in Santo Domingo, Dominican Republic. Sánchez received his formal art training at the Art Lyceum and the Institute of Bellas Artes in Santo Domingo. He moved to New York in 1962, and in 1982, Sánchez was offered his first children's book manuscript to illustrate: *Abuela's Weave*. Since then, besides his fine art painting, he has illustrated many children's books. Today, Sánchez and his wife, Joan, make their home on the Gulf Coast of Florida, where he continues to paint and illustrate.

SILVA, SIMÓN

Simón Silva was born in Mexicali, Mexico, and immigrated to the United States when he was one and a half years old. He is one of eleven children and grew up as a migrant student, traveling across California and Oregon, and as far north as Washington State to work every summer. Silva has become a very well-known artist, author, and speaker, and he travels around the country doing creativity workshops, keynotes, and presentations to students, parents, educators, and businesspeople. Read more at www.simonsilva.com.

SOTO, GARY

Gary Soto is the author of many poetry collections, short stories, plays, and more than two dozen books for young people. Soto's poetry and prose focus on everyday experiences for Chicanos. He has received many awards for his work as a children's author, including awards from the National Education Association and the PEN Center. He is a recipient of the Tomás Rivera Award.

TONATIUH, DUNCAN

Duncan Tonatiuh is both an author and illustrator. He has five picture books published by Abrams Books for Young Readers. He has won multiple awards and honorable mentions for his books and illustrations, among them the Pura Belpré Award, the Tomás Rivera Mexican-American Children's Book Award, and the Jane Addams Book Award. Tonatiuh received a Pura Belpré Honor for illustration for *Funny Bones: Posada and His Day of the Dead Calaveras*. He became the first Latino to win the Sibert Informational Book Medal for the same book in 2016. Tonatiuh grew up in San Miguel Allende in central Mexico. He graduated from Parsons the New School for Design and from Eugene Lang College in 2008. His work is inspired by ancient Mexican art, particularly that of the Mixtec codex. His aim is to create images that honor the past but that address contemporary issues that affect people of Mexican origin on both sides of the border. For more information visit www.duncantonatiuh.com.

VELÁSQUEZ, ERIC

Eric Velásquez was born in Spanish Harlem and grew up in Harlem. He graduated from the High School of Art and Design and earned his BFA from the School of Visual Arts. He wrote and illustrated *Grandma's Gift*, for which he received the 2011 Pura Belpré Medal for Illustration. He has illustrated numerous other books, including Beverly Naidoo's award-winning *Journey to Jo'Burg*, *The Piano Man* by Debbie Chocolate, and *The Sound that Jazz Makes* by Carole Boston Weatherford. The new book *Beautiful Moon*, written by Tonya Bolden and illustrated by Eric Velásquez, has gathered rave reviews and has been nominated for an NAACP Award. This is his fourth nomination. For more information, visit EricVelasquez.com.

Pura Belpré reads to children at the New York Public Library.
Center for Puerto Rican Studies. Hunter College, CUNY.

Index

Index

107

Index

"Lucky is the child [...] that finds the public library and discovers its picture books or reading hours."

The Stories I Read to the Children:
The life and writing of Pura Belpré, the legendary storyteller, children's author, and New York Public librarian.
Center for Puerto Rican Studies, Hunter College, CUNY

Credits